HYDROPONI
G

The complete guide to grow food and herbs at home!

(Hydroponic Techniques and Greenhouse System,

written by: © Louis Murphy

HYDROPONICS FOR BEGINNERS

GREENHOUSE GARDENING

HYDROPONICS FOR BEGINNERS

The complete guide to grow food and herbs at home!

(Hydroponic Techniques, Aquaponics System,

and Greenhouse Gardening)

written by: © Louis Murphy

Introduction

Hydroponics is the practice of growing plants using only water, nutrients, and a growing medium. The word hydroponics comes from the roots "hydro", meaning water, and "ponos", meaning labor, this method of gardening does not use soil. Instead of soil, hydroponic gardeners use different types of growing media, like coconut coir, vermiculite, perlite, and more.

In a nutshell, the idea behind hydroponics is to remove as many barriers as possible between a plant's roots and the water, oxygen, and nutrients it needs to grow (and thrive).

This can be done in many different ways, which is why we'll look at the different types of systems you can use to grow hydroponically — but first, let's understand the benefits and downsides of growing without soil.

It's important to keep in mind that you only enjoy this benefits if you set up and maintain your hydroponic garden carefully.

The biggest downside of hydroponics is the cost of buying a system.

Another negative is the experience required to run a system successfully. It's not THAT hard, but it is certainly more difficult than growing the same plant in soil. This is because you are creating an artificial environment where you provide the water, nutrients, light, and everything else the plant needs — which means you also need to monitor those inputs.

Types of Hydroponic Systems

- Wick Systems

- Deep Water Culture (DWC)

- Nutrient Film Technique (NFT).

- Ebb and Flow (Flood and Drain)

- Aeroponics

- Drip Systems

Wicking Systems

A wicking system is the most basic type of hydro system you can build. It's been used for thousands of years, though it wasn't considered a hydroponic system back then.

It's what's known as passive hydroponics, meaning that you don't need any air pumps or water pumps to use it.

Nutrients and water are moved into a plant's root zone via a wick, which is often something as simple as a rope or piece of felt.

One key to success with a wicking system is to use a growing media that transports water and nutrients well. Good choices include coconut coir, perlite, or vermiculite.

Wick systems are good for smaller plants that don't use up a lot of water or nutrients. Larger plants may have a hard time getting enough of either via a simple wick system.

Benefits of Wick Systems
- Truly "hands-off" if you set it up correctly

- Fantastic for small plants, beginner gardeners, and children

- Downsides of Wick Systems

- Not good for larger plants

- Incorrect wick placement or material can mean death for your plants

Deep Water Culture (DWC) Systems

Deepwater culture is hands-down the easiest type of hydro system to use.

In a DWC system, you use a reservoir to hold a nutrient solution. The roots of your plants are suspended in that solution so they get a constant supply of water, oxygen, and nutrients.

To oxygenate the water, you use an air pump with an air stone to pump bubbles into the nutrient solution. This prevents your roots from drowning in the water — a weird thing to think about, but it can (and does) happen to many beginner hydroponic gardeners.

Your plants are typically housed in net pots that are placed in foam board or into the top of the container that you're using for your reservoir. With some hydroponic growing media added into your net pots, they provide a home for the very beginning of your root system and plant stems.

Benefits of Deep Water Culture

- Very inexpensive and easy to make at home

- Extremely low-maintenance

- Recirculating, so less wasted inputs

- Downsides of Deep Water Culture

- Does not work well for large plants

- Does not work well for plants with the long growing period

The Nutrient Film Technique is a popular commercial hydroponic system.

Plants are grown in channels that have a nutrient solution pumping through them and constantly running along the bottom of the channel. When the solution reaches the end of the channel, it drops back into the main reservoir and is sent back to the beginning of the system again. This makes it a recirculating system, just like a deep water culture.

Unlike deep water culture, your plant's roots are not completely submerged in an NFT system — hence the "film" part of the system's name.

Plants are placed in these channels using net pots and growing medium and can be replaced or harvested on a one-by-one basis.

Benefits of Nutrient Film Technique
- Minimal growing medium needed

- The recirculating system means less waste

- Downsides of Nutrient Film Technique

- Pump failure of any kind can completely ruin your crop

- Roots can become overgrown and clog the channels

Ebb and Flow systems, which are also known by the name Flood and Drain, are a less-commonly seen system. But they're still quite effective and can be the best choice depending on your situation.

Unlike the previous two hydro systems we have covered, an ebb and flow system does not expose the roots of your plants to the nutrient solution constantly.

Instead, you grow in a tray filled with a growing medium. The tray is "flooded" with your nutrient solution a few times per day, depending on factors like:

The size of your plants

The water requirement of your plants

The air temperature

Where your plants are in their growth cycle

Flooding is accomplished by using a reservoir below the tray, a water pump, and a timer to schedule the flooding cycle.

After the tray is flooded, gravity drains the solution back down into the reservoir, where it is being oxygenated by an air pump and air stone. It sits there waiting for the next flood cycle, and the process goes on.

Hydroponic growers choose ebb and flow systems for their flexibility. Most of them will fill the tray with a growing

18

medium of their choice and also add net pots to organize their plants and control the roots a bit more.

Benefits of Ebb and Flow

- Efficient use of water and energy

- Highly customizable to your specific needs

- Downsides of Ebb and Flow

- Roots can dry out quickly if environmental conditions are off or the pump or timer fails

- Uses a lot of growing medium

Aeroponics Systems

Aeroponic systems are the most "high-tech" hydroponic setups that you can build. But they're not that complex once you understand how they work.

An aeroponic system is similar to an NFT system in that the roots are mostly suspended in the air. The difference is that an aeroponic system achieves this by misting the root zone with a nutrient solution constantly instead of running a thin film of the nutrient solution along a channel.

Some growers prefer to mist on a cycle like an ebb and flow system, but the cycle is much shorter, typically only waiting a few minutes between each misting. It's also possible to mist continually and use a finer sprayer to ensure more oxygen gets to the root zone.

Aeroponic systems have been shown to grow plants even quicker than some of the simpler systems like deep water culture, but this has not been verified to be true in all cases.

If you want to experiment with this system, you will need specialized spray nozzles to atomize the nutrient solution.

Benefits of Aeroponics

- Roots often are exposed to more oxygen than submerged-root systems

- Downsides of Aeroponics

- High-pressure nozzles can fail and roots can dry out

- Not as cheap or easy to set up as other methods

Drip Systems

Drip systems are extremely common in commercial operations but less common in recreational gardens. This is because they're simple to operate a large scale but slightly overkill for a smaller garden. Regardless, they're a great way to grow hydroponically that you should consider.

Benefits of Drip Systems

- High level of control over feeding and watering schedule

- Less likely to break

- Relatively cheap

- Downsides of Drip Systems

- May be overkill for a smaller garden

- Fluctuating pH and nutrient levels (if using the recirculating system)

- High waste (if using the waste system)

Hydroponics offers amazing flexibility, so even if you're experiencing some troubles, you should have no problem correcting them and getting your plants back on track.

Chapter 1: How Does Hydroponics Work?

The hydroponics system works by allowing you to control the basic environmental factors necessary for plant growth, such as pH balance, temperature, and monitored exposure to water and nutrients. The principle of hydroponics is simple - satisfy plant needs when they need it. All plants have unique nutritional needs. In hydroponics, therefore, your aim is to provide nutrients specific to the needs of each plant. Among other things, you get to control how much light the plant stays exposed to and the duration. You can also monitor and adjust the pH levels. By customizing and controlling the growth environment, your plants have a higher chance of growing faster than in a normal soil setting.

Another benefit of controlling the growth factors in the environment is that you avoid or reduce many of the risk factors that plants are exposed to in a normal growth setting. In fields and gardens, plants are exposed to a lot of variables that affect their growth and health. Animals (wild and domestic) plunder the ripe fruits and vegetables from the garden for their nourishment and fungus, pests, and diseases affect the plants' life by creating uncertainty. Locusts, for example, can wipe out an entire plantation in hours. With hydroponics, you can reduce these challenges considerably and do away with the unpredictable nature of plant growth outdoors.

Seedlings grow and mature faster in hydroponics because there is no mechanical resistance from the soil. You don't need to use pesticides, so your plants grow healthier and deliver a high yield of top-quality vegetables and fruits. Natural growth in the soil is awesome, but it comes with a lot of obstacles for plant growth and survival. When you eliminate these obstacles through hydroponics, your plants can grow rapidly.

A successful hydroponics system requires a few components. Below are three of the important components necessary to help you run a successful hydroponics operation:

- Growth Media

In hydroponics, you grow plants using inert media to support the weight of your plants and their root structure. Since you are not using soil, you need appropriate growth media. It is important to note here that the growth media you choose will offer no nutritional value to your plants. Its role is to absorb nutrients and moisture from the nutrient solution and release it to the plant.

Growth media should be pH-neutral. This is important so that they do not interfere with the pH balance in the nutrient solution. There are different growth media that you can choose for your plants. The ideal choice depends on the unique plant's needs and the type of hydroponics system you are using. You can find different growth media in online gardening stores or local nurseries.

- Air pumps and air stones

One of the most important factors you should consider is proper aeration. Without this, your plants could easily drown. This is where air stones and air pumps come in handy. Air stones contain dissolved oxygen. When immersed in water, they disperse the oxygen into the reservoir in your nutrient solution. The oxygen bubbles then distribute dissolved nutrients evenly within the solution.

On their own, air stones cannot produce oxygen. You must have them attached to an air pump. The air pump, on the other hand, has to be opaque to prevent algae growth. You can get air pumps and air stones in your local aquarium or pet store.

- Net pots

A net pot is a mesh planter used to hold your plants. The planter allows plant roots to grow from the bottom or side of the pot. This growth freedom exposes the roots, allowing easy access to nutrients and oxygen. Compared to conventional plastic pots or clay pots, the drainage capacity of net pots is unrivaled.

The Advantages of Hydroponics

There are a number of factors you consider before choosing a new way of doing things. The same applies to hydroponics. From your perspective, as a grower, the main factors you think about are quality of produce, yield, and efficiency. However, these are not the only benefits you stand to enjoy when working with hydroponics. You need to think long-term. Below are some of the benefits of using hydroponics:

- Overcome soil challenges

Hydroponics allows you to grow plants anywhere, whether you have limited access to soil, the soil is toxic, or you don't have access to growth space at all. On the same note, you don't have to worry about most of the challenges you normally experience with growing plants in soil, such as pests and diseases. A lack of access to arable land should not stop you from growing plants anymore.

- Maximize location and space utility

Everything your plants need is available and maintained within the hydroponics system. Because of this, you can grow the plants anywhere, even in your spare bedroom, as long as there is sufficient space to set up. Plant roots do not need to stretch and expand to find oxygen and food. Everything they need is available in the nutrient solution provided. This also means that you can grow your plants close to one another without worrying about space allocation.

- Freedom from climate constraints

One of the benefits of hydroponic growing is that you have full control over the important climate conditions, such as air composition, intensity of light, humidity, and temperature. This allows you the freedom to grow plants throughout the year, no matter the prevailing weather conditions in your area. In case you are a business farmer, you can produce plants at opportune moments during the year to maximize your profit potential.

- Save on water consumption

Another benefit of using hydroponics is that you get to save water in the process. This system uses around 10% of water compared to normal soil growth. Other than that, you recycle and reuse runoff water back into the system. The only way you lose water in this system is through evaporation or if you have a faulty hydroponics system that leaks. Considering that ground agriculture is responsible for most of the surface and groundwater consumption, switching to hydroponics is a brilliant idea.

- Nutritional value

Since you are fully in control of the nutrients that your plants need, there is little room for nutrient wastage. You can research the plants you want to grow and their nutritional needs at each stage in their growth cycle, then use this information to provide sufficient nutritional cover. Since the nutrients are contained within the growth tank, there is no loss through absorption into the soil.

- Controlling the pH

Each crop has a specific pH level at which it thrives. All the minerals you need in hydroponics are in the water. Therefore, you can make adjustments to the pH levels of water based on the mixture you need for each plant. This way, you provide the necessary nutrients without upsetting the pH balance.

- Faster growth

Compared to plants grown in the soil, hydroponics plants grow faster. You control all the growth conditions necessary for your plants. This way, you can provide the ideal condition for plant growth down to the finest detail. Since plants no longer have to struggle for nutrition, the energy that would be spent is channeled toward fruit production and optimum growth.

- Weeds, pests, and diseases

One of the challenges you deal with whenever you are growing plants in the soil is weeding. Weeds can be quite a headache in that they choke your plants, and at the same time, consume a lot of your time. Since weeds predominantly thrive on soil, doing away with soil in hydroponics eliminates the weed problem for you.

Other than weeds, without using soil, your plants are no longer at a high risk for pests and diseases, such as Pythium and Fusarium. You also don't need to worry about an invasion from locusts, birds, or any other pests. By controlling the growth environment, your risk of these deterrents is much lower than someone who is growing through the normal method.

- Limited use of herbicides and insecticides

Your exposure to pests and diseases is drastically reduced in the absence of soil. This also means that your use of chemicals in the growth process is also limited. As a result, you have a higher chance of growing healthier plants. The need for food safety at the moment is at an all-time high, and since hydroponics allows you to cut down on herbicide and insecticide use, it is a good alternative for gardening.

- Time and labor intensity

You save a lot of time and labor through hydroponics in terms of cultivation, watering, tilling, and other tasks necessary. The techniques used in hydroponics will also save you on the cost of repair and maintenance for equipment.

- Aesthetic appeal

The aesthetic appeal of hydroponics growth is another benefit you will appreciate. You can take care of your hydroponics farm easily without worrying about wandering through large fields. You can grow anything from fresh vegetables to herbs, fruits, and flowers and relax in the beauty before you.

The Disadvantages of Hydroponics

While there are many benefits of using hydroponics, it is not always an easy experience. There are challenges you might face in the process that you should be aware of. Preparing adequately for these challenges increases the prospect of success for your venture.

- Considerable investment

Each time you discuss an alternative way of doing things, it is common to assume costs will be affordable. However, this is not always the truth. A hydroponic garden needs a lot of your time, and in some cases, money. In a traditional soil garden, your plants will grow on their own, fend for themselves, and so on. There is little else for you to do concerning their growth. On the other hand, a hydroponic garden needs constant attention and considerable knowledge about what to use, how to use it, and when.

In a hydroponic garden, your plants depend on you for everything. From the initial installation, you must take care of the plants until they mature. If you plan on expanding the growth of your plants to commercial purposes, a simple water culture system might not be sufficient. You have to consider investing in an active system, which means buying pumps and other appliances. You will also need to automate the process. Automation calls for maintenance and considerable checks all around.

- Knowledge and technical experience

There are a lot of types of equipment you will use when running a hydroponic garden, especially for commercial purposes. You must know the growth process for each plant, the requirements and adequate light conditions, how far it should be away from the light bulb, and so on. Without this technical knowledge, you might struggle to raise a successful hydroponic garden. It gets more challenging when you are growing more than one plant species. You must know the fine details about each plant and factor it into the nutrient solution.

- Electricity and water challenges

Two of the most important elements in your hydroponic garden are water and electricity. A hydroponic garden does consume less water than a typical soil garden. However, you are constantly running a system in which water and electricity are in close proximity, and this creates a huge risk. You must have adequate safety measures in place, particularly if you are running a commercial operation. Other than that, you need a backup plan in place in case of blackouts. If your plants go without water for a long time, the roots will dry out.

- Initial cost

Depending on the expected size of your garden, your initial setup cost might run into a few hundreds of dollars or even higher. Some of the equipment you need include growth media, nutrients for each plant, a timer, pump, and lights. However, once your setup is complete, the only things you will have to spend on are electricity bills for lighting and running the water system and the cost of nutrients.

- Spreading diseases

One of the benefits of hydroponic gardens is that you don't have to deal with the conventional challenges involved in growing a typical soil garden, especially pests and diseases. However, there is always a risk that any disease that affects your plants could escalate to other plants within the same nutrient reservoir. However, this should not be a big problem for you, considering that the likelihood of diseases affecting plants in a hydroponic garden is so low.

For beginners or small home growers, you hardly need to worry about pests and diseases. However, if you are running a large hydroponic farm complete with greenhouses, a disease management plan will help you prepare for the uncertainty. For instance, you must check your hydroponic systems regularly, use sources of water that you are sure are free of diseases, and check to ensure your growing materials are free of diseases too. In the unlikely event that diseases happen, sterilize the nutrient solution, the infected water, and the entire system as soon as you notice the problem.

Why Should You Start a Hydroponics Garden?

Having learned about the hydroponics system, how it works, the advantages and disadvantages, why should you follow through and set up your own hydroponics system? When you come to think about it, people have grown plants the normal way in the ground since the beginning of time. Why should you go against the norm and start hydroponics farming?

For a fact, the benefits of hydroponics over traditional farming are incredible and widely documented. Considering the inherent challenges in traditional farming you might face, it makes sense to shift to hydroponics for your gardening needs. Hydroponics allows you the benefit of growing plants in places where traditionally, it would be impossible to grow plants. If NASA can grow plants in space, you can grow plants anywhere.

Let's take a look at a country, such as Israel, for example. Israel is predominantly an arid area. Naturally, it would be impossible to grow plants in this climate. However, Israelis produce a wide variety of fruits and vegetables through hydroponics. The same can be said of Arizona. Using the knowledge of hydroponics, residents can produce not just the food they need but also expand their operation and export the surplus.

If you are living in a typical urban area, you are aware of the challenge of land use and access. Getting available land for agriculture in urban centers is a problem, and where it is available, the land comes at insane premiums. Since there is little or no space available to plant a garden, hydroponics comes in handy.

If you live in a remote area, you can grow the plants you need all through the year. You do not need to worry about seasonal plants and vegetables or the challenges involved in importing produce. If you live in an area where you don't receive a fair amount of consistent warmth, such as in Russia or Alaska, your growth seasons are much shorter than in other places. Hydroponic greenhouses can help you get to produce all year.

The environmental impact is another reason why you should consider hydroponic gardening. Compared to traditional soil-based gardening, you save up to 90% on water using hydroponics. How is this possible? In hydroponics, you can recycle and reuse not just water but the nutrient solutions too. This is very beneficial in places that have acute water shortages.

As to the effect on the environment, hydroponic plants only need around 20-25% of the fertilizers and nutrients that you need in normal soil gardening. You also need little or no pesticides at all. This means that hydroponics gardening doesn't pressure the environment as much as traditional gardening would, and while at it, you enjoy significant savings. Since you don't need to import products anymore, the other benefit to the environment is a reduction in greenhouse gas emissions through transportation. You also spend a shorter time harvesting plants grown through hydroponics because their root system is not so elaborate. All the nutrients they need are readily available. Considering all these factors, investing in hydroponics is a brilliant idea.

What do your plants require?

Both plants need the right conditions to reach their full potential. Plants grown by systems of hydroponics are no exception to this fundamental rule. As their soil relatives, they require adequate light of the appropriate wavelengths, an adequate temperature, adequate supply of water, enough oxygen, mineral nutrients and structural support.

An adequate light of the right wavelengths is important for the plant's survival at its growth stage. Plants use a lot of light every day, at least 8 to 12 hours, to generate carbon dioxide and water. The green color of plants, chlorophyll, absorbs the sunlight and uses its energy to synthesize these carbs.

This process is called photosynthesis and is the basis for the survival of life in all plants. As animals and people eat plants, it can also be viewed as the source of our lives. Artificial lighting is generally a poor substitute for sunlight as most indoor lights do not produce a mature crop in sufficient intensity.

High intensity lamps such as sodium high-pressure lamps will supply over 1000 foot light candles. The hydroponic gardener can very effectively use these lamps in areas where sunlight is not adequate.

Nevertheless, the machinery and lamps are typically too costly for a small commercial company to operate. It is essential that there is ample spacing between plants, as this ensures that every plant gets enough light in the growing room.

For example, plants of tomatoes cut into one stalk must be planted to give 4 square feet per plant, while seedless cucumbers of 7 to 9 square feet and seeded cucumbers of approximately 8 square feet must be permitted in Europe.

The salad plants must be 7 to 9 centimeters apart in row and 9 centimeters between rows. Most other vegetables and flowers should be planted at the same distance as for the traditional greenhouse.

For the plant to grow normally, a suitable temperature is needed. Too high or too low temperatures can cause an irregular development and decreased performance. Summer and most flowers are best grown between 60 ° and 80 ° F, while winter vegetables such as spinach and lettuce tend to have temperatures between 50 ° and 70 ° F.

Appropriate water is usually not a concern in the use of a hydroponic system, since water containing solution nutrients is the basis of hydroponics. However, there are some systems that can cause insufficient watering, with the resulting adverse results for your plants.

Ebb and flow systems not tested on an appropriate basis can run short of nutrients, as can continuous flow systems in their storage tanks. Most, if not all, automated hydroponic systems can have catastrophes unless closely monitored.

Blocked or burst pipes or pump failure can lead to a lack of nutrient flow, resulting in dry roots and severe damages to or even deaths of your plants together with extreme lighting and the appropriate ambient temperature in the growing room.

Oxygen is a fundamental requirement for most living things. Plants require breathing oxygen to take water and nutrients. There is normally enough oxygen in soil environments, but plant roots in water use the supply of dissolved oxygen quickly.

This may harm or even destroy the plant without the provision of additional air. The bubbling air through the solution is a common way of ventilating the nutrient. Continuous flow and aeroponic systems typically do not require additional oxygen.

Many green plants require mineral nutrients. To order to survive, they must consume certain minerals from their roots. Such minerals are provided by the soil and the application of fertilizers such as manure and compost in modern horticulture.

The large quantities of nitrogen, phosphorus, potassium, calcium, magnesium and sulfur are required and only very small quantities of nitrates, iron, manganese, zinc, copper, molybdenum and chlorine are needed.

The soil surrounding the growing plant normally provides support. Nevertheless, a plant grown with hydroponics must be artificially assisted. Typically this is achieved by string or stakes. You can buy cheap automatic string rollers to help your plants as they grow. This reduces the tedious task of continuing to adjust strings in rapidly growing plants.

Pest Control In Hydroponics

When you're using hydroponics to do your gardening, you don't have the same risk of pest infestation that you do when outside. However, you probably still have some concerns about protecting your plants from pests. It's a good thing to be vigilant, but it's even better to prevent a pest problem before one happens. So here's what you need to know about hydroponic pest control:

The Most Common Pest Problems in Hydroponics

If you want to control pests, you first need to know what you could be dealing with. Here are some of the pests that you're most likely to find if you've got pests in your system:

- Aphids

A lot of people are familiar with aphids from school lessons, and here you thought you were done with them. But they do infest hydroponic systems, especially when your plants have too much nitrogen in their food source. They're usually found around the plant stems and these little guys can be either black, green, or grayish/tan.

- Whiteflies

Whiteflies can be tricky, but you can spot them pretty easily. They look like tiny white moths (about 1mm long) and fly away as soon as you're about to catch one.

- Spider Mites

Spider mites are even smaller than whiteflies, at under 1mm in length. And they're definitely one of the most dreaded infestations of a hydroponic system. They do look like tiny spiders, but since they're so small they can easily escape notice until an infestation gets way out of control.

- Fungus Gnats

Fungus gnats are another tricky pest since the grown gnat isn't harmful but the larvae are. You'll find the pest larvae eating at roots, which can bring on bacterial infections pretty quickly.

- Thrips

Thrips, like aphids, can turn leaves yellow or brown because they suck the nutrients out. They're a little bigger at 5mm, but still hard to spot. They'll look like small, black dots on the upper sides of leaves.

Avoid Things that 'Invite' Pests into Your Growing Area

There are certain 'good practices' that can help reduce the chances of a pest making its home in your hydroponic system. Fortunately, a lot of these practices involve a little know-how and a bigger dose of avoidance. That means one of the best things you can do is avoid introducing opportunities that appeal to pests.

Don't Go in Dirty

Before you enter your growing area, you should be wearing sterile (or at least clean) clothes. All kinds of bacteria, pests, and other contaminants can cling to our clothing totally unnoticed. Even if you don't think there's anything there, just don't risk it. A pest problem is a high price to pay for skipping 2 minutes to get ready to enter your growing area. You're not done yet though, your tools and anything you bring into your growing area needs the same care.

Basically: don't bring anything into your growing area that isn't clean and contaminant free.

Give Your System a Sterile Start

If you're setting up your system or doing a little work on it, see the tip above. Even fixtures, vents, tanks, and any other gear needs to be cleaned before they're introduced into your growing area.

Period

Checking the quality of the seals around your growing area is important, too. While you want a well-ventilated area, you don't want a free for all for pests. Make sure there isn't an issue with seals on windows and doors to outside areas (especially when your growing area is close to outside vegetation).

Outside Materials

Pests can crop up from some sneaky places, and the materials you introduce into your hydroponic garden are an unassuming hiding place. The pest home that we inadvertently bring into our hydroponic systems?

Growing medium

Look, this isn't to create a scare campaign because the truth is most growing mediums are perfectly sterile, and safe. But there are some things to look out for. If you're getting an organic growing medium, such as coconut or rice husk, pay special attention. These mediums can harbor pests, so they need special treatment. Make sure that your growing medium has been sterilized, put through treatments to eliminate pests, and has some credible backing behind those claims.

New Transplants (take care)

Whenever you're planning on adding transplants into your system, you need to be careful. Outside plants can carry bacteria, fungi, diseases, and pests. To combat these risks, you need to get any transplants from a clean, well-maintained place you can trust. And before you go transplanting anything just because it came from a 'reputable' facility, take the time to examine the plants for any health issues.

The First Steps in Hydroponic Pest Control

Pest control can be something you start practicing with at the very start with your hydroponic system. Putting in measures that deter pests is going to be your first line of defense. Here are the best ways to prevent a pest problem:

Watch Your Humidity

Some pests, like spider mites and fungus gnats, are especially attracted to low humidity and excess moisture in other parts of your system. Keeping your humidity from getting too low (50% is a good level to keep plants healthy and keep mites away), can prevent an infestation. But it isn't all about your ambient environment. Keeping too much moisture from your growing medium can deter pests, like fungus gnats, from taking up residence (especially if you use rockwool, which they love).

How to Identify a Pest Problem

Even with diligent prevention, you can still have a pest sneak its way into your system. Like any hydroponic setup, you should be examining your plants for problems regularly. That being said, you don't want to confuse signs of pests with signs of other issues, such as nutrient deficiency or disease. Here's how to tell if your plants are suffering from pests or another ailment:

1.Discoloration

When pests suck the nutrients out of leaves (like aphids do), you'll notice that the leaves become discolored and often turn a yellow color. This discoloration is centered around tiny holes that the pests feed on, not just generally spread on leaves.

2. Spots

Some pests can leave a signature pattern of spots, whether white, yellow, brown, or black. If you notice spots, check to see if they're deposits on the leaves (from eggs, feces, etc), or actual damage to the leaves. If the spots scrape off, you can pretty well bet you've got a pest issue.

When you notice these on any plant, check the leaves and stems of other plants to determine the pest and the degree of infestation.

3. Holes from pests vs burns and lesions

When you first see a hole or rip, it can be easy to make assumptions. That's why it's important to look closer and check out the edges of any holes. Burns should be fairly obvious, as they'll appear where light and heat sources are close to plants and show discoloration around any holes or burns.

The pests that are most likely to infest hydroponic gardens are more 'suckers' than 'munchers.' That means the holes they leave from feeding on plants are tiny, and often raised and surrounded by a more yellow, or whitish area.

What to Do When You Have a Pest?

If you've noticed some of the above symptoms of a pest problem, you need to get it fixed and quickly.
Unfortunately, when a pest has already made its way in, it can be difficult to mitigate the issue. Pests can run through

a hydroponic system at a surprising speed, so once one
plant is affected the others tend to follow in short order.

Don't Wait to Take Care of a Pest

If you act immediately after spotting pests, you may be
able to spare the rest (or remaining unaffected) of your
plants. If you wait, you're probably going to come home to
a garden that's been almost, if not entirely, infested.

Determine the Level of Intervention Needed

 Some pests can be taken care of by changes to the
environment, manual removal, or other methods, while
some pests can only be banished with chemicals. Whenever
possible, avoid introducing harmful chemicals into your
hydroponic system.

More Gentle Methods of Pest Removal:

Sticky traps

One of the first things you can do, depending on the pest
you're dealing with uses sticky traps. These work like the
other sticky bug traps you're familiar with and can be
helpful especially with pests that have short life cycles.
Another bonus of using sticky traps is that it can help you
identify the pests infesting your system. If you can identify
the pests, you can take a more appropriate route to get rid
of them (even if sticky traps don't eliminate them).

Tip: Keeping sticky traps can be a preventative measure,
too. If you see pests caught in a trap you can prevent a
larger issue.

Natural solutions

A lot of solutions are marketed for killing pests, but you
don't want to chance to kill your plants too. When in doubt,
make sure your solution is backed with plant safe

guarantees. A solution you can rely on, without a doubt, is Pyrethrin. It sounds very chemically intense, but don't worry. It's been given the green light for even certified organic farmers to use, so you know it's safe. Pyrethrin is extracted from chrysanthemums and can put a stop to pests.

A Good Spray Down

Oftentimes you can give your plants a good hosing down to start getting pests under control. True, it won't kill all your pests, but it can disrupt another cycle of reproducing, and it'll get the bulk of them off your plants.

Hydroponic pest control: The cheat sheet

If you've found yourself with a pest problem that quickly becomes an emergency, here's the cheat sheet you need.

- Symptoms:

- Black spots on leaves – see Thrips

- White or yellow spots – see Spider Mites, Whiteflies, Thrips, Aphids

- Deformed stems or leaves – see Fungus Gnats, Aphids

- Deposits on leaves – for silvery streaks see Thrips, small black see Thrips, sticky residue see Aphids, white masses and clumps see Mealybugs

- Webbing around plants – see Spider Mites

Pest information and treatment

Aphids

Aphids secrete honeydew, a sticky residue that stimulates the growth of sooty mold (honeydew can also attract other pests such as ants). These creatures such nutrients out of leaves and can leave them looking yellow and crinkled.

Tell-tale signs:

Aphids leave behind a good deposit of honeydew when they're feeding, so you're unlikely to miss these deposits. You can usually spot the aphids moving around stems, although they can be a variety of colors.

Treatment:

You can use predator bugs that feed on aphids to control their infestation; ladybugs and lacewings are the most common choices. Safe soap pesticides contain different formulations, but most are safe for plants and deadly for pests. Leaves, stems, or even whole plants that are severely infected may need to be removed. Next, try not to overfeed your plants, as that will increase aphid problems.

Fungus Gnats

Adult fungus gnats are annoying but not a huge problem (aside from the fact that they reproduce). The larvae are going to be your real issue, as they congregate near and fed on the roots.

Tell-tale signs:

The first sign you may notice is the adult fungus gnats that fly up in masses whenever you disturb a nearby area. The larvae can be found by looking at the growing medium and turning it over a bit. The plants they feed on start by looking 'ill,' meaning they get yellow leaves, look wilted and seem frail.

Treatment:

First, avoid these guys by trying not to overwater your plants; but if you've already gotten to that point, try letting the growing medium dry out as much as possible, to a couple of inches from the surface before adding any more moisture. You can catch eggs with sticky traps near the medium, and introduce nematodes to take care of the larvae. Neem oil can also be sprayed for severe infestations.

Mealybugs

Mealybugs love fruiting plants, so if you're growing the like you're more likely to see them. These are another 'sucker' type of pest, so you'll notice weak, yellow leaves if an infestation becomes larger.

Tell-tale signs:

Mealybugs leave eggs in white, cottony looking masses on the undersides of leaves and stems (although they make be located anywhere on the plants). They leave behind a honeydew residue, much like aphids, and generally, have a waxy coating.

Treatment:

Solutions: you can treat Mealybug problems with a gentle, natural pesticide or insecticide. You can also use a solution of 1 oz Neem oil with 1 gallon of water and spray every 1 or 2 weeks until the infestation is gone. Some helpful insects such as ladybugs can also be used.

Tip: if you catch an infestation early, you can manually destroy egg sacks with a swab soaked in alcohol and then remove them.

Spider Mites

Spider mites leave fine webs all over plants and can be a difficult pest. They tend to infest areas with high temperatures and low humidity.

Tell-tale signs:

First, the webs. Spider mites leave behind sticky webs, just like regular spiders, but smaller and finer. Since they also suck nutrients from leaves, you may notice yellow and whitish spots on leaves. They can grow in number quickly before you notice webs, so check the undersides of leaves where they gather.

Treatment:

First, manually remove areas of high infestation by pruning and removing heavily infested leaves and stems. Then you can use a safe, organic insecticide or biological insecticide to get it under control. A mixture of Neem oil and a wetting agent (for the better spread) can also be sprayed every few days to kill mites and eggs.

Thrips

Thrips can grow huge populations in a short amount of time, and a heavy infestation can cripple a garden if left untreated. These hyperactive pests are especially attracted to light-colored plants and flowers.

Tell-tale signs:

One of the biggest signs that you've got a thrip problem is black spots on the leaves. The black spots are actually feces dropped onto leaves. You'll also notice that the plants they feed on get discolored spots and may appear dry.

Treatment:

The first thing you can do to get rid of thrips is to release some insects that feed on them. Lacewings and ladybugs are typical beneficial bugs, but minute pirate bugs are most effective when it comes to thrips. If the problem grows too large, pyrethrin can be used and followed with insecticidal soap when needed.

Whiteflies

Whiteflies hide on the undersides of leaves and look like miniature moths. Like fungus gnats, they fly up in large crowds when disturbed.

Tell-tale signs:

Like aphids, whiteflies leave a sticky honeydew residue that you can spot on leaves (as well as any sooty mold that's grown as a result). You may also see light, discolored spots where whiteflies have been feeding on leaves. Once an adult population has been established, you should be able to easily tell if they're in your system.

Treatment:

To begin reducing the infestation, spray plants with water at a moderate pressure, and begin introducing beneficial insects. Like most pests, you can use ladybugs and lacewings to reduce them, as well as the whitefly parasite. Organic soap insecticides can get rid of them quickly, as can spraying with Neem oil.

Chapter 3: Hydroponic System

What Are You Growing?

This is a major influencing decision because different plants are suited to different growing environments. If you are planning on growing a few vegetables, then a smaller system will do, but if you want to grow more then, you will need a larger system. If you are planning on growing plants that need different conditions, then you are likely going to need multiple systems or one where you can grow the plants in pots rather than in the same conditions as everything else.

Considering what you are going to grow before you buy your hydroponic system is necessary to ensure the best outcomes from your hydroponic system. So, choose a plant that should meet your requirements. For example: if you have less space, then you can choose to grow some herbs or vegetables that generally need less space as compared to other plants. You can quickly grow some herbs or vegetables on your patio or balcony for family consumption.

Flowering plants need a unique combination of nutrients, pH, and minerals, so use a bigger hydroponics system that can hold enough of the single flower plants. If you want to grow hydroponics for commercial purpose and you have an ample space, then use different combinations of hydroponics that suit the plant you wish to grow.

Before you start shopping for your hydroponic system, you need to understand what you are going to grow and how much of it.

Will It Fit?

Considering the space that you are going to use for your hydroponics is another primary consideration. You must measure your space to fit your hydroponics system properly. You should seek to use your space effectively so that your hydroponics get enough sunlight and air through the day for proper growth. This step becomes mandatory when you are using a patio or balcony for your hydroponics.

Most systems come with the dimensions listed on them, but if you are building hydroponics from scratch, then take a tank that should fit your space correctly. Choose a container that fits in your space and also leaves some space around the area so that you can maintain your hydroponics easily. Some large plants hang over the side of growing tanks, so you must consider that point before buying a hydroponic system.

When determining the size of the system, you need to consider accessibility too. There is no point having a system that is so big you cannot get around it and access your plants and equipment.

If you are growing in an attic, then you need to consider the size of the entrance and whether the tank will fit. As roof height is a major consideration in attic rooms, you may want to buy growing systems that are low to the ground so that there is plenty of room for the plants to grow upwards.

How Noisy is the System?

You may initially think this is a minor consideration, but when you have to live with the system constantly making noise all day long, you may suddenly give this point more thought.

For larger systems, you will need a larger pump which means more noise unless you are making your system up from multiple smaller units.

One thing to consider is when the pump will be running during the day. If it is loud, then you are not going to mind the noise during the day when you are at work, but running it at night is going to disturb you and your family. An NFT system needs the pump on virtually 24 hours a day whereas a flood and drain system is okay if the pump if on for a few minutes every two or three hours.

This is a hard judgment to make, and it is worth visiting a store and looking at the different pumps to hear how noisy they are for yourself before making your decision.

Cost

Your budget is another primary consideration for you while choosing a hydroponic system. Many hydroponic systems like aeroponics come in ready-made kits, but they are usually expensive to buy and maintain as well. So, if you need a hydroponic system that will suit your budget, then you can buy some parts and assemble them on your own.

Water culture hydroponics is a better option for you if you need an affordable hydroponics system that you can easily build on your own. All you need is to buy some common items like a water tank, air stone, bubble maker, a few cups to plant the system, gravel-like stone or sand, etc. Some of these items are readily available around your house and you can use them in a hydroponics system.

 Make a list of what you need for a hydroponics system and check whether any items are already available at your home. Do some research on the price of these items online and offline and choose the things that suit your budget.

This is a major part of the decision-making process for many people. There are pre-made systems for pretty much any budget, but for someone who really wants to do hydroponics on a budget, then you are looking at making your own system from components or spare parts.

Most people are going to start with a smaller system and then when they get hooked on this hobby either increases the number of systems they run or buy a bigger system!

Shopping around and looking online will help you to save some money as you will often find better discounts from online retailers.

Electricity and Other Running Costs

Most hydroponics systems need electricity to run the air bubbler. You should also need a heater to control the temperature of your hydroponic if you are living in cold weather areas. You will also need a lighting system that requires electricity. There are also other considerations like maintaining the nutrients in your solution, replacing the solution, replacing growing medium etc. that you should bother about. If you think that your hydroponic is not cost-effective, then you can switch to a different hydroponic system. However, this should not be your concern if you are building hydroponics as a hobby.

The majority of hydroponic systems are going to use electricity to power the pump and sometimes a nutrient heater in the cooler months to keep the nutrient solution at the right temperature. For year-round production, you will need lights, which will use more electricity.

On top of that, you have to consider the other running costs like water, replacing the growing medium, nutrients and so on.

Can you Leave Your Hydroponic System?

Most hydroponic systems can be left unattended for a few days, depending on how big your nutrient reservoir is compared to the water needs of your plants. If you want to leave your plants for any length of time, then you will need a good-sized nutrient container.

In most cases, you will change your nutrient solution around every two weeks and top it up every four or five days. The pH of it will need adjusting, and this can be done when topping it up.

Time and Manpower Needs

Different systems need different levels of attention from you. Some of the most expensive operations are mostly automated, meaning that you don't need to do as much, whereas other systems require more frequent manual intervention. Will you be using pots or not?

Some of the growing systems allow you to grow in pots, which is excellent as you can use different growing mediums and adjust 'soil' conditions for individual plant requirements. This is helpful for when you get started as you can grow a variety of different plants rather than only one type.

The method of setting up your hydroponics system varies with the type of hydroponics system you want to build. Hence, we would be treating them one by one.

Ebb and flow

Ebb and Flow hydroponic crops (or even Ebb and Flood, flow and reflux) are slightly more complex in design, but extremely versatile. This system works by alternating a filling phase of the culture substrate and an emptying phase.

A submersible pump and a timer regulate the flow of water and nourishment, which first invades the substrate where the roots rest and then is discharged back into the tank below.

One of the major advantages of the ebb and flow hydroponics is the possibility to further customize the irrigation program based on the size of the plant, the number of plants, temperature, humidity, etc

In this type of hydroponics, the chamber that the roots develop in appears as a cylinder like channel that is set at a slight slope so the nutrient arrangement will move through it. These frameworks regularly comprise of different developing channels in light of the fact that there's a breaking point to what extent a solitary channel can be for down to earth reasons and before nutrients begin to get exhausted at the far end.

The plants are arranged in openings in the highest point of the developing channel, so the roots are suspended over the nutrient arrangement inside the chamber while the crown reaches out above. There's frequently no requirement for a developing medium, with NFT hydroponics, other than net pots to help the plants.

The arrangement is siphoned from a store to the higher finish of the developing channel, and in the wake of moving through the length of the channel, it's come back to the supply. Nutrient film technique hydroponics is in this manner a shut framework that reuses the nutrient arrangement, permitting you to save water and nutrients.

Necessary Equipment

- Tank with lid

- Plant growth tray to be placed above the tank

- Rubber hoses

- Water pump with timer (the pumps for garden ponds work perfectly)

- Plants grown in an inert substrate (which can be coarse sandy material, clean gravel or rock wool cubes).

Instructions

- With the drill, drill two holes on the lid of the tank and make two more on the base of the tray where the plants will grow, perfectly aligned with each other.

- Connect a couple of holes with a drain pipe, one of the ends of which must come out into the tray above the water level expected to collect the excess water (if the flood levels are too high).

- Connect the other pair of holes with a black tube, which will act as both a flood pump and a drain.

Attach one part of this tube to the pump immersed in the tank and slide the other out into the growth tray.

- Place the pots with plants inside the tray. The heights of the pots should be twice that of the edges of the tray.

- Set the pump timer. To do this, configure a flood period of 15 minutes and a drainage period of another 15 minutes.

How often should I flood and drain the tray? This depends on the substrate you use and the climate. In colder climates, or with substrates that drain more slowly (such as stone wool), two floods per day should suffice. In warmer climates, or with substrates that drain more quickly, up to four floods per day, if not six, should be fine.

And that's how much! If you are looking for an easy-to-use plant with which to immerse yourself in the world of hydroponics, the ebb and flow system may be part of your future.

Hydroponics with Wick

Wick systems are the simplest system from the mechanical point of view and the easiest to install. This is because hydroponics with wick does not require movement at all.

The plant sprout is placed in a container with substrate (sand, gravel, perlite etc.) and placed above a tank with water and nourishment. The container and tank are then connected with a wick of cloth or rope, immersed on one end in the ground and on the other in the water.

The capillary action of the wick fiber causes the water full of nutrients to rise towards the culture medium, where it is absorbed by the roots of the plants.

The hydroponics with wick is excellent for learning the basics, but it may not work well with large plants or in need of a lot of water (the wick cannot supply large quantities quickly)

Instructions

- Fill a jar or small bucket with nutrient-rich water. Ideally, the container should be slightly smaller in circumference than your growing pot, and opaque. The container will act as a reservoir to supply water and nutrients to the plant.

- Take the pot you intend to use for your plant and place both wicks in the center. There need to be a small hole in the bottom of the pot so that the wicks can pass through.

- Fill the pot with the growing substrate, making sure that the wicks are of a big enough length such that they easily contact the roots of the plants.

- The length of the wick may require some adjustment. When you are satisfied you can place the plant pot on top of the container of point one. The pot containing the plant must now be suspended above the water, with the wicks partially submerged.

To prevent pests or contamination, make sure the tank is sealed. You want to prevent air and light from coming into contact with your liquid solution.

So you just made your first hydroponic wick system! It is now necessary to observe the level of the solution in the tank to check when it needs to be refilled. The time between refills varies according to the thirst of the plant.

Hydroponics with DWC System

This is the cheapest, but simplest to set up a hydroponic system for a beginner to grow on a small scale.

Your plants having access to nutrient-rich and hydrogen peroxide for 24/7 obviously means that your plants will grow very fast. In fact they will grow faster than in most other hydroponic systems because a flow system is followed. Follow the flow of the system means that the roots of your plants are constantly exposed to nutrients, which lays the foundation for strong curve growth. Obtaining larger plants is easier because of this growth acceleration

The main drawback of DWC is temperature regulation: in any hydroponic system, it is important to keep your nutrient solution fresh at seventy degrees Fahrenheit. This is done so as to ensure the oxygen level stays optimized.

However, in the DWC hydroponics system, this is very important as your plants are always in contact with nutrient solution. This can be problematic if you live in a warmer climate.

Another disadvantage is that maintenance can be quite burdensome:

• You need to change the water very reguarly so as to keep the nutrients and the water fresh. Also, you will have to do it manually.

• To prevent malnutrition of your plants, it is also important to check the water pH value regularly. Also, check the nutrient content of the force / profile with a water meter. PPM and most importantly, adjust the pH and / or nutrient strength profile when things are out of balance.

But even with these inconveniences, DWC is probably the best hydroponic system to start if you are a beginner and you will only grow from 2 to 6 plants.

Great, here are some things that I highly recommend:

- DWC Hydroponic Bucket Kit 5 Gallons, 6 inches;

- DWC Romper Cube Kit by PowerGrow Systems. (4) 5 Gallon - 6 " Cubes;

- DWC Romper Cube Kit by PowerGrow Systems. (8) 5 Gallon - 6 " Cubes;

- Of Deep Water Recirculation Cultivation System. (4) 5 Gallon Buckets + 1 Control

In a system like this, you do not have to check each individual cube for pH or ppm values, because there is no single bucket control that the nutrient arrangement streams. Also, this will spare you some time. Each segment can contain a single plant. To get as many buckets as the number of plants we are going to grow.

Drip Hydroponics System

Drip irrigation systems are relatively simple in how they work.

If you are a beginner to hydroponics, the sophistication of this system makes your installation and maintenance less simple than that of the previous systems. But more on this later.

This is the way this system works:

Allow your plants to be placed in a medium that is inert. Such mediums include rock wool and stones.

Rich in nutrients, water is pumped from the nutrient tank to the top of its culture medium.

After this, allow nutrient rich water to drip slowly from pipes or tubes connected in a network. The slowly dripping water would then drip to the plant's roots.

A drip irrigation system follows a flow system, which means that it is easier to get your plants from FAST growth.

As a beginner or novice, one thing to realize is that a system like this is very delicate and can go bad anytime. Hence, you need to be well prepared.

For starters, if you are in the DIY, the creation of a drip irrigation system takes more time and attention to the installation of the previous systems (Flow and Reflux or DWC).

Then there is the danger of obstruction of the emitters and potentially ruin their growth ... if not that the water is maintained and / or emitters free of nutrients accumulation.

It is also necessary to find the perfect balance in how much to expose the roots of your plants drip / flow irrigation. Dripping too easily can lead to root or fungus rot ... while too little can result in stunted growth.

Finally, if your energy goes out for whatever reason and your pump stops leaking, you basically have only a couple of hours to notify

Drip irrigation systems are the most efficient way as before (Flow and Reflux systems and DWC). Proper installation of drip irrigation system requires less water and less nutrients than Flow and Reflux or DWC.

General Hydroponics Aeroponic System

Aeroponic systems are one of the most expensive and sophisticated of all hydroponic systems.

If all right, it is also the system with the will to give the greatest rewards in terms of production, and is the most efficient in terms of water and nutrients.

Here's how it works:

- Its plant roots are sitting in a dark chamber closed circuit;

- Small drops of the nutrient solution in an atomized form nutrient solution get periodically sprayed on your plant roots while they sit in this dark and closed chamber;

- As drip irrigation and DWC systems, this also follows a flow system. And because oxygen levels are so high it has the potential to overcome the performance of other types of hydroponics. They are more difficult to maintain and relentless in case of errors.

- As with the drip irrigation system, with an airplane system, it is extremely important that you keep the sprayer clogged.

A couple of hours of blocked complete sprayers can kill your whole crops. In cleaning your aeroponic system, ensure everything is clean before you put it into the system:

filters, tubes, pumps, etc. You can get some high quality nutrients like those from General Hydroponics. The low quality of nutrients can leave that the residue salt has not dissolved, which is bad news for your sprayers. Also, ensure that you keep the temperature of the nutrient and moisture solution at the root of the chamber at optimal levels:

•Nutrient solution: 64 ° F

•Moisture in the root zone: 100%

•Moisture in the growth zone during veg stage: 60-70%

•Moisture in the growth zone during flower stage: 30-40%

If you do not keep your temperature and humidity levels on the check, there is the risk of things like root rot, algae and slowing down the growth of plants in general.

It is one of the most rewarding hydroponic systems there is.

Although the aeroponic system is the most risky and least suitable hydroponic system for beginners on our list, it is also the system with the highest performance with the fastest harvest cycles.

If you decide to go for an aeroponic system, you really advise me to start with a pre-made system like: *"General Hydroponics Selva 66 Aeroponic System"*

To create a home NFT system you can use different materials that can be from specialized products to items that can be found in the home and recycled for this project.

A simple way you can do it is with the following materials:

4 PVC pipes of 4 and half meters long;

3 4-inch PVC elbows;

1 plastic canister with a capacity of 20 liters;

1 fish tank pump from 3 thousand to 4 thousand L / H;

1 hose half inch and 3 meters long;

8 screws (to fix the tubes);

20 small disposable baskets or glasses 5 centimeters in diameter;

20 seedlings of lettuce;

Nutrient solution for 20 liters;

Teflon tape (to hold the hose)

The first step is to drill the tubes to place the baskets where the seedlings will go, each hole must be at a distance of 20 centimeters. Then the PVC elbows are placed to join each tube, already attached they are placed on the wall and marks are made to place the screws.

The second step is to place the screws on the wall 2 in 2 at a distance of 1 meter long between each pair, so that they are zigzag. The important thing is that the tubes have an inclination of one degree so that the nutrient solution and the water can circulate easily and does not stagnate.

The next step is to place the PVC pipes on the screws to distribute the baskets with the seedlings inside each hole.

The fourth step is to fill the plastic canister with the nutrient solution diluted in water; After the pump is introduced and connected to the hose that will go in the highest tube, the hose is sealed with the Teflon tape and the canister is placed under the last tube so that the water falls into it and is not wasted. Finally, the pump is connected to make the system work.

Growing Seedlings and Early Vegetables on Peat

This is probably the cheapest and yet very successful option for growing plants without soil. Many amateur gardeners who have hotbeds will certainly breathe a sigh of relief when they learn that they do not need to spend time and energy on acquiring suitable manure. In addition, in this case, good compost soil is not needed, because the work is done with clean peat chips.

We will deepen the bottom of the greenhouse or forcing bed so that it is 15 cm below the soil surface, and then, without resorting to the help of a film, we will fill the entire space with pre-treated peat crumb. In this case, pre-treatment means adding 2 kg of slaked lime per 1 cubic meter, thoroughly mixing and moisturizing the entire mass of peat. A frame filled in this way can now be planted with seedlings or sown seeds. All vegetables will feel well and grow quickly under glass if we regularly water them with a good nutrient solution. (Do not forget to cover the reservoir with the solution with bituminous paint!) After feeding the solution, immediately irrigate it with clean water, which is used to wash all parts of the plants to remove the residual solution. Don't just forget that this time, there is no film under the peat crumb layer, and therefore, the excess solution can freely seep into the subsoil. Therefore, it is advisable to always spend only as much solution as necessary so that the peat crumb always remains moist, but never is saturated with moisture.

The list of devices worthy of attention for commercial applications of soilless plant growth does not, in any way, end with a description of distillation ridges. Both professional and amateur gardeners have discovered a host of other possibilities for applying the method, with which you can usefully use its advantages. It is simply impossible to list all of them, so we will combine them into groups and indicate what the matter is in each case.

Using the opportunity to supply plants with approximately optimal amounts of water and nutrients and creating habitat conditions for them in which they will feel good (it's worth remembering, for example, root respiration). Plants will thank us, as practice shows, with earlier, more abundant, and higher-quality products.

Saving labor costs, which we no doubt - and this is easy to see - we can use for our own benefit or pleasure.

Let us come up with other options and methods for growing plants commercially without soil, and dare to the first independent experiments. The main provisions to be reckoned with are known to us. Of course, there may be setbacks, but they will also benefit us, because, no doubt, they will teach us a lot.

Plant Material

We have many opportunities for obtaining the plant material required for planting, namely:

- we can transfer plants grown in a traditional way to soilless culture - with a lump of soil;

- you can use plants grown in the so-called standard soil, that is, in a mixture of sterile subsoil clay with difficult to decompose organic impurities;

- you can sow seeds in a substrate;

- plant propagation by cuttings can be carried out in one of the substrates known to us.

Preparatory Work

It is clear that you cannot sow seeds in large gravel. Therefore, first, you need to pre-process inorganic substrate, whether it is fine gravel, coal slag, or other materials, sorted into particles of the appropriate size. We need fractions with the following particle diameter: For cultivation vessels 4–15 mm for the incorporation (dusting) of small seeds 0–2 mm or for propagation by cuttings of 2–3 mm.

To obtain these fractions, we sift our stock of substrate and store each of the obtained fractions separately. We throw out the passage or the smallest dust, and grind large particles and sift again. All obtained fractions of the substrate must be sterilized.

Sterilization of the substrate is an extremely important operation. You can never predict which pathogens of plant diseases or harmful microorganisms come in the form of a free application with a substrate if it is not sterilized. The sterilization process is very simple: potassium permanganate (a well-known disinfectant) is purchased in the nearest pharmacy and a dark red solution is prepared. Gravel is poured into this solution for a day, making sure that it is completely covered with the solution. After a day, the solution is drained, the gravel is thoroughly washed with clean water, and you can be sure that our pets will not receive unwanted companions - the gravel is disinfected!

Such sterilization must be carried out whenever a culture is removed and the vessel or unit is cleaned for a new culture. Apart from peat chips, all other substrates can be used again and again for growing plants. Used peat will find good use in the garden. Thanks to each sterilization, we ensure a healthy start to the next culture.

The amount of gravel that is intended for sowing seeds or for propagation by cuttings, we, shortly before use, additionally treated with a highly diluted boric acid solution. This somewhat stimulates the growth of roots, and therefore, and the entire plant. Boric acid (H_3BO_3) is sold in pharmacies in powder or tablet form. The solution is prepared in a proportion of 1:10 000, that is, 1 g of boric acid is required per 10 l of soft (rain) water. This solution is poured once with gravel for a wiring culture and the excess solution is allowed to drain since excess boron is undesirable and even harmful.

If wooden boxes are used for propagation by cuttings, then they are lined with a thin plastic film to make them waterproof. Metal or asbestos-cement boxes are covered with bitumen paint from the inside, and the paint must be allowed to dry completely before starting work with the box: the solvent poisonous to plants should completely disappear.

Flower pots, which will subsequently be used for pickling seedlings or planting rooted cuttings, are likewise sterilized in a solution of potassium permanganate, especially if they were already in use.

In conclusion of our preparatory activity, we must still etch the seeds with any of the recommended preparations, as is usually done when growing plants in the soil. When sowing seeds and when propagating plants by cuttings, the use of growth substances is quite acceptable, and here it is necessary to adhere to company regulations. However, in this case, the substrate should not be treated with a solution of boric acid, since it cannot be predicted in advance whether the simultaneous use of both agents will adversely affect. Let us turn now to the plants themselves.

Transfer of Plants from Soil to Nutrient Solution

We agree on the principle: here we are talking exclusively about an auxiliary solution, which, however, might have to be used very often. Currently, there are still few flower and vegetable farms in which seedlings grown without soil could be purchased. Therefore, obviously, it is necessary to learn how to transfer plants to new conditions for them.

It must be borne in mind - and this is why we are talking about a forced decision - that such a transfer is an unnatural event, in which, even with extreme caution, one cannot help but damage the root system of plants to one degree or another. Therefore, we use seedlings of plants with not yet very strong lump and delicate roots. Transplanting old plants is not recommended: only a few of them will undergo this operation painlessly since a large loss of roots slows down or even completely stops all further growth. However, if for some reason, it turns out to be desirable to transfer the old specimen to the aquatic culture, you need to act more than carefully and immediately prune the aerial parts of the plant in proportion to the loss of roots.

Transfer to aquatic culture is carried out in the following order: in the evening, the day before, seedlings or young plants are placed in a basin with water, which should cover the pots with seedlings through the top so that the lump of land is completely saturated with it and, therefore, loosened. The next day, having prepared a large amount of water heated to 35-37 degrees, the roots are lowered into it and very carefully and if possible completely remove the soil adhering to the roots. In plants with a rough root system that tolerates not too delicate handling (for example, monstera, ficus, etc.), this is easy to do. On the contrary, the fine-fibered root system, which is characteristic of gloxinia, peperomia, etc., requires very careful handling to save the plants from painful growth arrest.

Ordinary garden soil should be removed as carefully as possible. The fact is that it contains a significant proportion of easily decomposable organic components, which, with a relatively abundant supply of water in plants or vessels without soil, quickly decompose and become a noticeable obstacle. Add to this that, over time, shallow soil forms a sediment at the bottom of the installation, which can adversely affect the smooth operation of the pump.

For seedlings grown in the so-called standard soil, there is no need to equally thoroughly clean the soil. The lump, in this case, does not contain any rapidly decomposing substances, and therefore, it is enough to remove that part of the soil which itself is easily separated, and the lump residue firmly held by the roots can be left without any hesitation. However, when planting such plants in gravel in the pit around the roots, a little fine gravel should be added (as a filter) so as not to endanger the pump.

Plants released from the soil should not be left lying for a minute; they should be immediately planted in the intended place. Plants are planted in the same way as in natural soil, but they should not be squeezed, as this leads to crushing and deformation of the roots. Instead, try to "wash" the substrate onto the roots. Small vessels, for example, water pots, flower boxes, etc., that can be moved, are filled with water to the top for this purpose. Put an internal pot or section in them and lightly tap them on the edge of the external vessel. In this case, gravel, for example, in flower boxes, settles by almost 2 cm. This ensures better contact of the roots with the substrate.

In larger plants, we wash gravel with a strong stream of water from all sides towards the newly planted plant. Of course, all excess water is then removed from the tank.

In a series of hydroponic vessels, most of the root system of plants is freely immersed in the solution. Here, we carefully plant the plants in a substrate layer on the grate, while at the same time, we try to pass individual roots through the grate to the level of the solution in the tank. If necessary, the substrate after planting is moistened again.

Even with a very caring attitude, damage to the roots can never be completely avoided. Therefore, the transplanted plants are put in the shade, in a cool place where there is no flow of strong air, leaving them there until they recover. About when this will happen, we learn from the renewed growth, swelling (turgidity) of all types of tissues, and, in general, the whole appearance of the plant. Until this time, transplanted plants do not receive any nutrient solution, but only water. Damaged areas of the root system cannot tolerate any salt-containing solutions and must first be tested.

Transferring plants to aquatic culture will not cause difficulties for a true lover. With fairly delicate handling and some skill, this task can be successfully dealt with. However, it is much more advisable to go the natural way and propagate plants also without soil.

Growing Seedlings from Seeds without Soil

We already have waterproof seedling boxes. Before filling them with a substrate, in one of the corners, we put a small flower pot with a slightly larger hole against the usual bottom. It will serve to control the level of the nutrient solution and to replenish its loss. The largest fraction of the substrate is poured into the bottom of the box with a layer of about 2 cm. The smallest fraction, as well as in soil culture, is used to sprinkle seeds. The nature of the substrate should correspond to the size of the sown seeds. Asparagus seeds can, for example, be planted in coarse gravel, but lettuce seeds require the smallest fraction of gravel.

A Simple Method of Propagation by Cuttings

For rooting cuttings, seedling boxes are prepared in the same way as for sowing seeds. It is highly desirable that, in this case, the boxes are a little deeper. Then in the future, it would be possible to create a small supply of nutrient solution in the box and reduce labor costs, and the cuttings themselves would not have contact with the liquid.

All other work is carried out in exactly the same way as in ordinary soil culture. Moderation is required when watering since excess water easily causes decay and mold.

After sowing the seeds and before their germination, and when rooting the cuttings to the formation of roots, moistening is carried out only with clean water, since nutrients are not required before the indicated development phases. However, it is then necessary to begin plant nutrition. Boxes with seedlings are filled with normal nutrient solution up to half the height (following this on the control pot), and in the boxes cuttings for the first time are served the same solution, but diluted 10 times. The fact is that the need for already rooted cuttings at first is still small and, in addition, the not-yet-sampled cut points in weaker cuttings will not be damaged if the solution concentration is low. Depending on the speed of rooting of cuttings, which proceeds very differently between different species and at different times of the year.

The rule for determining the desired level of nutrient solution is as follows: the roots should not "bathe" in the solution. Therefore, you need to start with such an amount of solution that its level reaches half the height of the substrate, and then gradually lower this level.

How often should a nutrient solution be added? Water evaporates faster than the nutrients it contains are consumed, and therefore, an undesirable increase in salt concentration is possible if only the nutrient solution is added all the time. Remember the following simple calculation: 1 g of nutrient salts is sufficient for the formation of 30-35 g of plant matter. Therefore, if we, for example, poured 3 liters of a solution containing 3 g of mineral salts, then plants can form 90-105 g of plant tissues (aboveground mass and roots) from this. Based on this, we can always approximately determine the extent to which the existing salts are used and whether it is time to add a new portion of the nutrient solution or is it more important to add only water.

Seedling Care

Here, the groundless method can especially reduce labor costs. We can place thousands of young plants planted in pots in one large flat bath or shelf and supply them all with a solution from one point completely automatically. The advantage of the method of periodic flooding, namely, the change of air in the mass of the substrate, becomes especially evident in young plants demanding oxygen.

Our need for seedlings will probably not be so great as to necessitate a special plant for growing it. Amateur gardeners who have built themselves a miniature plant of the above system can now rejoice because such is excellent for growing seedlings. The only thing required is to remove the upper third of the substrate layer and immerse the pots in the remaining mass so that their edges remain at least 1 cm above the maximum possible liquid level.

A smaller part of the pots can be placed in waterproof seedlings in which seeds were sown and rooting cuttings. The space between the pots is filled with gravel. In the corner, as before, set an empty control pot through which water and solution are supplied. In accordance with the phase of plant development, you need to change the liquid level in the box so that the roots are not immersed in it.

When caring for young plants, one should not lose sight of an important point: ordinary flower pots with a drainage hole in the bottom always have to be placed at least on a thin layer of gravel to ensure absolutely free flow. If you put such pots directly on the film, there is always the danger of too tight contact, and then the drain of the liquid will be much more difficult. In some places, pots with drainage holes on the side surface are already being produced, and they should be preferred for this case.

Stages of Development of Plants on a Hydroponic Plantation

As noted, usually, the propagation of plants on hydroponic plantations begins with the cultivation of cuttings by layering or aerial shoots. What is after this? Let us take a quick look.

Vegetative Stage

Most plants remain at the vegetative stage if exposed to illumination for 18 hours a day. To start the ripening process, the daylight hours should be reduced to 12 hours. It is best to grow short plants. Any lamps are less intense than sunlight.

It is best to transplant cuttings with developed roots, give them a couple of days under 18-hour lighting for vegetative growth with appropriate nutrition. Then, continuing to give vegetative nutrition, it is necessary to reduce lighting to 12 hours. Suppression of the vegetative stage results in stunted plants. It seems strange to strange people, but overgrown plants look much worse with bare long stems resting against a lamp.

As soon as you change the light mode, the pre-flowering stage will begin. For a couple of weeks, the plants will still fill the space and form an excellent crown, but at the same time prepare for flowering. After two weeks, growth will stop, and the plants will remain dense, shortened, using all the advantages of lighting. Extra branches that are not illuminated must be cut. It is the branches, not the leaves.

This stage of plant development is the simplest, since you no longer need to do anything, and only observe the ripening of the plants. If the stages of rooting and vegetative growth are passed successfully, the plants will turn out healthy and give a plentiful harvest. For the ripening phase, you only need to choose the ideal diet, which is not so simple.

When ripening, the plant ages and begins to fade, it loses the lower leaves and expends energy to reproduce. This process must be accompanied by a special balance of nutrients. There are plants that are left without leaves, others are green to the very end. Excessive nutrition can lead to premature ripening. The nutrition schedule is individual for each type of plant.

When flowering begins, the need for food changes dramatically. The solution should be changed and the nutritional composition changed. In the process of ripening, changes in nutrition are no longer required. You can arrange a "rinse", leave clean water for plants for 2-3 days, or you can do the opposite - increase the nutrient content, while plants absorb less water, a little stress does not hinder them.

The food schedule can be very different. Some plants do not need two weeks for vegetative nutrition, others are in no hurry to ripen, and still, others ripen too quickly. If you need to grow plants for seeds, you need at least one male for pollination. Nutrition is the same as when growing flowers.

Lighting is essential to plant growth and plays a key role in deciding plant yields. Hydroponics growing equipment manufacturers therefore integrated a wide range of lighting device designs to meet specific requirements of various plants grown indoor growing rooms.

Lighting requirements vary, depending primarily on the type of plant, the environment where the plants are grown and the proximity of the plant to the light source. The most important consideration is the lighting level a plant needs for healthy growth.

Some plants like houseplants and ferns require less light than salads and culinary herbs, while tomatoes, orchids and flowering plants require maximum lighting.

It has been found that indoor growers appear to under-illuminate their indoor growing rooms as they try to cover an area with the available light. We need to understand the importance of adequate lighting, bearing in mind that a smaller area adequately lighted would yield better results than a larger area with insufficient lighting.

Fluorescent Lighting Fluorescent lamps are ideal for small-scale salad and herb gardens and seedlings and cuttings. Fluorescent lights are ideal for slightly larger plants as T-5 fluorescent bulbs are approximately equal to 400 watt Metal Halide light in PAR.

Such lights must be kept near plants on all sides, but wonderful plants with short internode distances can grow as long as the plant is not too big. T-5s are best for vegetative growth.

High Intensity Discharge Lighting

Vegetables, trees, and several other plant varieties do their best with all the light they can get, and the new HID lights do their best. HID lighting has evolved from a piece of equipment to an almost "plug and play" lay person use with improvements in lamp and reflector design.

HID lights come in two types, remote ballasts and integrated ballasts. The remote ballast design has the advantage of suspending only its lightweight reflector unit from the ceiling; the integrated design requires suspending the entire unit, including the heavy ballast.

HID lighting comes in two basic types — Metal Halide and Sodium High Pressure. Metal Halide HID lighting produces blue white light and is recognized as particularly well suited for overall plant growth, whereas high-pressure sodium producing red / orange light is better suited to flowering and fruiting periods during which plants can use it more readily.

All types of HID lighting are used with growers either alternating the two by plant growth cycle or combining the two throughout the crop. Nonetheless, the latest design of sodium lamps now available in the "Agro" or "PLANTA" range can provide the light energy required throughout the plant growth cycle and are increasingly used by skilled growers.

HID lights range from 250 to 1000 watts and beyond. The lamp that provides optimum light output is the 600 watt sodium lamp, generating 92,000 lumens.

Reflector

While it is important to use the right lamps to produce the correct amount and type of light, it is equally important to ensure light is focused in a manner that minimizes waste. Reflector design plays an important role in optimizing light utilization; a well-designed reflector can be as efficient as 30% as a poorly designed reflector in terms of its ability to reduce light loss.

The most efficient reflectors generated using computer-aided modeling techniques in market feature designs. These designs maximize plant light reflection and enhance lamp life.

1. In addition to effective light reflectors, rail systems allowing lamp movement to ensure light exposure to the most remote plant go a long way in improving light utilization. A rail system called the Light Rail 3.5 has proven particularly effective in increasing light efficiency, and those with a rectangular growing area will consider it.

This is a simple device that uses a six-foot rail with a precision engineered carrier that moves back and forth across the growing area.

The Light Rail 3.5 system offers many advantages-it covers a larger area and guarantees that all plants receive the same amount of light; it removes the shifting of plants for light exposure and reduces shadows, ensuring uniform plant growth.

It also allows plants greater exposure to light without burning the leaves. Certain systems that shift the light along a circular path are more suitable for square-growing spaces.

Many systems also require combination lighting on one arm with a Metal Halide Lamp and a High Pressure Sodium on the other, or 4 different ceramic bulbs on 4 separate arms, each giving different color temperatures. Such 4 separate bulbs, when combined via a revolving or rotating light mover, combine to create a very full spectrum.

2. Reflected Light

Reflective surfaces around the growing area will change the amount of light plants receive. Low surface reflectivity around a plant can decrease the amount of light as surfaces absorb most of the incident light. Ensuring highly reflective surfaces around plants in a growing room isn't difficult.

Walls can be conveniently painted with flat white paint, an outstanding reflector. If not, the walls can be covered with black / white plastic film that can also be used for the floor. Polystyrene foam sheeting can also be used as a strong surface reflecting.

The most reflective cover is brilliant white vinyl. It's tough and hard, making a reflective surface perfect. Finally, MYLAR, the most reflective material, will reflect 92 percent of the light it receives.

3. Timers

Manual lighting on and off requires the use of a powerful timer. When implementing a timer in the lighting system, the plants in the growing room are exposed to light for the "on" set time after which the lights are turned off for the "off" set time.

Continuous, continuous repetition of this on / off cycle is essential; a reliable, high-quality timer is critical. It is best to avoid ordinary non-grounded plug-in timers as they are vulnerable to failures that interrupt flowering cycles in some plants and increase power bills.

Power Consumption Power consumption is one of the factors to consider when working on the project's economics. This should not, however, discourage the beginner as the costs involved are surprisingly small. The beginner should first work out the power requirement and economics to avoid problems later.

Alert Grow-rooms can be humid. To avoid contact with water splashes, all electrical equipment, fittings and accessories should be carefully marked. Helping a licensed electrician when building the electrical system is advisable.

Chapter 6: Best plants for Hyroponics gardening and nutrition

Are you wondering what plants you can grow hydroponically indoors if you don't have much space? Hydroponics, or the method of growing plants in nutrient-rich water rather than soil, can be used to grow a wide range of vegetables, herbs, and other plants, but some plants are better suited for this soil-free growing method than others.

Below, we take a look at 10 nutritious vegetables, herbs and fruit plants that are among the easiest plants to grow hydroponically at home. These plants will also adapt to aquaponics, an advanced hydroponic growing method that combines aquaculture (raising aquatic animals such as fish) with conventional hydroponics. While the small aquaponic herb growing kits available for consumers won't allow you to raise fish for food, they do have the advantage of fertilizing your plants with the natural waste the fish produce in the tank below the grow tray.

1.Spinach

The health benefits of spinach make this leafy green vegetable a great addition to almost any healthy diet, but the unassuming spinach is also right there on top of the list of the best plants you can grow hydroponically at home. Not only does spinach grow well in most water-based gardens. You can harvest your hydroponically-grown spinach all at once, or snip off a bit at a time. The young leaves of the spinach plant make a particularly versatile ingredient as they can be eaten both raw and cooked.

2. Lettuce

Lettuce may well be the most popular choice among budding hydroponic gardeners. It is easy to grow, and you can keep harvesting the outer leaves as the plant grows and thereby benefit from a continuous supply of fresh lettuce. Don't know which variety to pick? Try the extra healthy Romaine, or any other common leafy type, such as the Bibb.

3.Watercress

As the name implies, watercress is a water-loving plant that makes an ideal candidate for your hydroponic or aquaponic garden. It is also a great vegetable to grow at home as it doesn't store well when cut, which means the watercress you find in the grocery stores is often already wilted. This semi-aquatic plant thrives best in water that is slightly alkaline and that keeps moving.

4. Cherry Tomatoes

Cherry tomatoes are one of the easiest non-leafy vegetables to grow indoors at home, and they also do well in hydroponic systems. Keep in mind, though, that tomatoes, including cherry tomatoes, require a lot of light to grow, so you might want to get a standalone grow light, or one of the cherry tomato growing kits with LED grow lights.

5. Cucumbers

The cucumber plant is another example of a food-producing plant that grows well in a hydroponic or aquaponic setting, provided that it gets enough sunlight or artificial light designed to boost plant grown. When planting cucumber vines, keep in mind that as the plants grow, the vines will likely need to be supported with a large trellis or wire cage. No room for vines and a large trellis? Popular among container gardeners, the bush types are much smaller than the more common vine types, and you can buy bush cucumber seeds conveniently through Amazon.

6. Peppers

Like tomatoes and cucumbers, peppers are relatively easy to grow indoors at home, provided that they get a lot of natural sunlight or that their growth is supported by grow lamps. They are also well-suited to hydroponic cultivation. If you're planning on setting up your hydroponic garden in your home, rather than in a large greenhouse, you might want to consider opting for chili peppers and other smaller pepper varieties that are better suited for small spaces than bell peppers.

7. Kale

In recent years, kale's health benefits have received a lot of media attention, and cookbooks focused on kale recipes abound. However, fresh kale is still not as readily available as many other vegetables, and non-organically grown kale is often laden with pesticides. By growing your kale using hydroponics or aquaponics, or simply using soil as the growing medium, you'll have fresh kale readily available. Plus, if you're growing your kale in a controlled hydroponic system indoors, you will likely need no pesticides as planet-destroying bugs living in soil or flying around outside will have trouble accessing the growing plants.

8. Strawberries

Imagine if you could have fresh, locally-grown strawberries indoors all year round! With a well-designed hydroponic system, year-round cultivation of strawberries becomes easy as pie. To get started, purchase a couple of strawberry starter runners from a garden supply store, and place them in a refrigerator for a few months before planting them in your hydroponic indoor garden. Such cold stimulation helps jump-start the growing process, and your strawberry plants should start producing flowers right after planting.

9. Mint

Although it is usually grown on land, orange mint (also known as water mint) is a semi-aquatic plant that in nature grows best in shallow water on the sides of ponds and streams. Also, peppermint, which is a hybrid cross between spearmint and orange mint, loves water. Therefore, it is not surprising that both orange mint and peppermint are among the best herbs to grow hydroponically or aquaponically, even if you have no prior experience in hydroponic gardening.

10. Basil

Basil is another example of a herb that is easy to grow in a hydroponic system. The easiest way to get started with growing basil in a hydroponic system is to buy basil seedlings at a garden center and transplant the seedlings into the hydroponic container after carefully rinsing the soil off the roots.

The Essential Nutrients

Nitrogen

Nitrogen is one of the principal elements that contribute to a plant's growth. Plants use nitrogen to create amino acids and proteins that are used to generate new growth in cells. Nitrogen quickly travels throughout the plant to promote new growth at the detriment of the older foliage. Any deficiency will cause weakness in the new growth and spindly result in a stunted plant. The shortage is usually first noticeable in older leaves of a plant which lose their green color and gradually turn yellow. This is because nitrogen is essential in the leaves for the green oxygen which produces chlorophyll pigment.

The small leaves will also be yellow as the scarcity persists and the veins on the underside of the leaves turn a red or purple colour. Vegetable plants may run to seed. An abundance of nitrogen will also affect the fruiting or seed production of most plants

Phosphorus

Another essential plant growth factor, phosphorus, is also crucial for plant photosynthesis and cell forming. It acts as a catalyst facilitating energy transfer for the plant, in this case. Phosphorus is important in the development of good root systems, and is also needed to form the flowers and seeds of a plant. Because phosphorus, like nitrogen, is very mobile within the plant, any deficiency is usually visible in the color of the plant's leaves. Deficiency of phosphorus produces a deep green colouring of the leaf.

Potassium

Potassium, like phosphorus, acts as a catalyst for activating or triggering a number of plant functions within plants. It is a source for plant enzymes that ward off disease and play an important role in the development of cells.

The mottling of older leaves on plants and yellowing of leaves along their veins may suggest a deficiency in potassium. It is another item in the plant that is mobile so the older leaves first display any deficiencies. Plants which lack this nutrient may lose their fruit before it matures.

Calcium

Calcium is the element that supports cell walls as they form in plants. It helps buffer other elements ' excesses, and is an important part of the root structure of a plant. Calcium in plants is not very mobile so it is present in older growth in greater concentration. As a result, when there is a calcium deficiency it is the new growth which first suffers.

The older growth preserves its calcium but this important element will be short of new growth. The fresh tips of the leaves and the rising points tend to die back with a calcium deficiency and the leaves have a brown to black scorching, even low calcium is the source of blossom end rot, often seen as a black scab on the tomato fruit bottom.

Magnesium

Another factor essential for photosynthesis in plants is magnesium. It is vitally important for the chlorophyll molecule and is also widely used in seed production. A deficiency can yellow in the leaves of a plant and spread from the center to the outer edges of the leaf. The leaves eventually turn an orange colour. A lack of magnesium gives rise to further issues if you want to grow additional plants from the seeds being produced as they are malformed and have a poor germination rate. Magnesium acts as a phosphorus carrier within the plant and encourages the formation of oils, fats, and juice.

Sulphur

As with calcium, sulphur is important in the tissue structure of a plant. It is one of the plant protein components and plays an important part in producing most plants ' flavors and odors. When the younger leaves on a plant become pale, a lack of sulphur appears. Despite continuing growth, it tends to be hard and woody with very little increase in radial growth. Within a plant, sulfur does not move around much.

Iron

Iron is required for chlorophyll production in plants and is used in photosynthesis. An iron deficiency will affect new growth of the plants, the leaves will become almost white and the leaf veins will show a definite yellowing.

Iron is not very mobile or easily absorbed within plants making it a problem element to replace once lost. Iron is an important micronutrient that all plants and animals need.

Manganese

Manganese is involved in many plant enzymes, particularly those which reduce nitrates before protein production. The mottled yellowing of younger leaves will generally characterize a shortage of manganese. Especially on citrus trees, only small, yellow leaves form and develop no further. It's also affected the formation of new bloom buds.

Zinc

Zinc is a part of growth hormones and is essential for most plant enzymes, too. Zinc is another element that once lost isn't easily replaced. The new, zinc-deficient plant leaves are highly undersized. Zinc increases the energy source for chlorophyll production, and also promotes water absorption. This is partly why plants which lack zinc may be stunted. Also partly dependent on the presence of zinc is the formation of auxins, hormones which promote growth in plant cells.

Copper

Plants use copper as an activator or catalyst for various important enzymes. A lack of copper will cause new growth to wane, or sometimes irregular growth, often with new shoots dying back. Sometimes, fruit can break during maturity, particularly at warm temperatures. Copper increases the sugar content of citrus fruit and makes crops such as carrots, spinach and apples more colorful. When haemoglobin is formed in animal blood, copper is important in the use of iron.

Boron

In this element, boron deficiency is generally shown by the slow death of plant tissue especially around the main growing point and the roots ' apex or center point. On the fruit of plants lacking in boron appear cracks varying from small to fairly large in size. Quite often the roots become hollow and deteriorate. As well as being important for pollination and seed production, boron is necessary for normal cell division and protein formation.

Molybdenum

Molybdenum is used by plants in the formation of proteins and affects the ability of the plant to fix atmospheric nitrogen. Pale leaves which appear burnt towards the edges may suggest a deficiency. Sometimes, the leaves may get distorted. Broccoli, Brussels sprouts, lettuce, cauliflower, and other brassicas will not adequately grow leaves when molybdenum is unavailable. Molybdenum is also essential for plants such as peas that use nitrogen fixing bacteria to have nodules on their roots. Only after detailing the functions of these nutrient elements can it be concluded that they are all vital to the production of healthy plants.

You may wonder how plants may thrive in the soil where in varying degrees one or more of those essential elements may be deficient. Plants grow extremely well in the wild, uncontaminated by humans. Only plants which are suitable for extremely poor soils will grow on those soils. In addition, plants gradually modify the soil by breaking it up with their root systems, some even help to replace nutrients in the soil, for example, peas have nitrogen-fixing bacteria in the legumes at their roots. Some plant species are bound to become established even in the most deficient soils, paving the way for other species which may succeed them later on.

Complex plant communities develop frequently, such as the New Zealand native forests, feeding large amounts of humus into the soil as old growth breaks down to make way for new growth. The native trees ' intricate root systems retain this fertile soil in place while the thick cover offered by their leaves keeps it moist and humid, creating the ideal conditions for ferns and other undergrowths.

If left alone, plants respond to their surroundings and change it very effectively, the difficulties arise when people try to support large numbers of people, set up complex monocultures. Single crop varieties are cultivated over large areas, allowing large-scale application of pesticides to remove rivals and other chemicals for disease control. The remaining humus in the soil from bygone native forests will soon be spent requiring ongoing large-scale fertilizer applications that may provide plants with the nutrients they need but do not replace the function of humus in keeping the soil in a light, aerated, workable condition.

During the construction process, the home gardener is put in a similar position on a new section that had all but the minimum amount of topsoil required to grow a layer of grass. Topsoil (and compost) must be returned to form a vegetable garden or fruit trees. It takes fertilizers and compost to bring up the humic content in the soil. However, the home gardener is hampered by the lack of technical guidance from the experts who are often employed to examine the soil conditions where substantial cropping is performed and recommend the appropriate fertilizer applications. Prevention is better than cure for the home gardener wanting to grow a variety of crops, the solution being to keep feeding a steady supply of fertilizer and compost into the vegetable garden soil rather than waiting for the signs of deficiency described earlier to emerge.

Hydroponic production reduces the issues associated with poor soil and is low in nutrients for commercial and domestic crops alike. Instead of spending large quantities of fertilizers on a large area of soil where crops are to be grown, the commercial grower can cycle the required quantities within a compact hydroponic system by adding more nutrients only as needed.

Hydroponic systems reduce the problems faced by home gardeners when a fertilizer added to one plant community counteracts another fertilizer applied to multiple nearby plants. It is also easy to nourish plants in large quantities. Some important factors need to be present in small amounts because too high a concentration can be toxic to plants. Excellent hydroponic nutritional products made for the crop being grown contain the right nutrients in the right proportions for optimal growth, and can be easily measured and measured with inexpensive, efficient and readily available equipment.

By adding humus to the soil, decaying plant matter also improves its condition. Some plant species are bound to become established even in the most deficient soils, paving the way for other species which may succeed them later on.

Complex plant communities develop frequently, such as the New Zealand native forests, feeding large amounts of humus into the soil as old growth breaks down to make way for new growth. The native trees ' complex root systems keep this enriched soil in place whereas the dense cover offered by their leaves keeps it moist and damp, giving the optimum conditions for ferns and other undergrowths.

When left alone, plants adapt to their environment and modify it very efficiently, the problems arise when people try to support large numbers of people, set up specialized monocultures. Single crop types are grown over large areas, requiring large-scale application of pesticides to eliminate competitors and other chemicals for disease reduction. The residual humus in the soil from bygone natural forests will soon be exhausted needing continuing large-scale fertilizer applications that may provide plants with the nutrients they require but do not substitute the role of humus in holding the soil in a warm, aerated, workable state.

Prevention is better than cure for the home gardener wanting to grow a range of crops, the solution being to keep feeding a steady supply of fertilizer and compost into the vegetable garden soil rather than waiting for the symptoms of deficiency described earlier to appear.

Hydroponic growth eliminates the problems associated with poor soil and is deficient in nutrients for commercial and domestic growers alike. Instead of spending large quantities of fertilizers on a large area of soil where crops are to be grown, the commercial grower can cycle the required quantities within a compact hydroponic system by adding more nutrients only as needed.

Hydroponic systems eliminate the problems faced by home gardeners when a fertilizer applied to one plant group counteracts another fertilizer applied to various nearby plants. It's also easy to apply too large a quantity of a nutrient to your plants. Some of the crucial elements only need to be present in small amounts as they become toxic to plants if they are present in too high a concentration. An excellent hydroponic nutrient food, tailor made to the crop being grown, contains the right nutrients in the right proportions for optimum growth and is easily measured and adjusted with cheap, efficient and readily available equipment.

Humidity

In order to maintain conditions suitable for plant growth in the, it is necessary to provide a number of parameters, the first of which is humidity. In conditions of high humidity, the leaves of plants grow larger. Their maximum growth is observed at 60-80%. But it is better not to stick to the extreme numbers and set the humidity at 65-75%. Cuttings will need more moisture - up to 90%, and 60% is enough for seed germination. During late flowering, it is best to use minimal humidity to avoid mold.

Humidity is a relative concept: there is much more water in hot air than in cold air. The used percentage humidity parameter is associated with water, which air is able to hold at a given temperature. This indicator is completely unrelated to the total water content in the air. At ten degrees and 100%, the relative humidity of water in the air will be half as much as at the same humidity, but at 20°C. This means that any increase in temperature in the room will lead to a decrease in humidity.

Accordingly, if the lighting turns off and the temperature drops, the humidity increases. So, darkening the room for the dark period of the cycle, it is worth running the hood for a few minutes to remove excess moisture. Otherwise, it will settle on the leaves in the form of dew and can serve as an environment in which pathogens multiply. If the lighting is on, the humidity drops, so do not immediately start the hood to keep CO_2 produced at night.

If the humidity has dropped below 40%, and the air outside is too dry to raise the humidity, ventilation is indispensable: you will need a household humidifier. The air outside is usually cooler than the one in the room, therefore, once inside, it heats up and loses moisture. So even if the air outside is initially humid, it is not suitable for increasing humidity in the greenhouse.

In cold weather, it is better to cover the ventilation so that the air in the room warms up. Plants produce a lot of moisture, so it is even possible to use a dehumidifier. Plants prefer stability, so sharp changes in humidity are best avoided. If the leaves are bent up, this may be due to a rapid loss of moisture, rather than an unbalanced diet, so do not rush to add corrective substances: it may be a matter of humidity.

Ventilation

Ventilation is needed, powerful and reliable, capable of updating all the air in the room in one minute. However, if the fan is too powerful, it will be difficult to ensure constant humidity. You can use an exhaust fan that can replace the air in the room in 4-6 minutes - this is enough, and the atmosphere will be stable in the room.

It is necessary to use different types of ventilation in parallel: an exhaust fan mounted on an outlet in the wall under the ceiling - it will blow air from the room; an outlet with an air intake located on the floor, in the opposite corner to the hood of the room, while the air intake must supply air from the basement or from the north wall of the house, it will not interfere with installing a protective net from dust and insects, if this does not interfere with the passage of air; circulation fans will make the air in the room homogeneous, exclude cold or hot abnormal zones, direct them better directly to the stems, which will allow air to be removed from under the crown, making the spread of diseases and insects more difficult.

The exhaust fan is calculated simply. The volume of the room in cubic meters is multiplied by 12 (updating every five minutes - 12 times per hour). The resulting figure is an indicator of the corresponding fan. But there can be various barriers to the airflow. Thus, a carbon filter significantly reduces fan performance if air from the outside enters through the pipe, each of its elbows is an additional obstacle. Too small air intake will reduce fresh air. All these factors can be taken into account by taking a fan with a performance 25% higher than the calculated one.

Carbon Dioxide

The plant feeds on sunlight while consuming the carbon dioxide needed for photosynthesis, during which the carbohydrate necessary for the plant is formed and oxygen is released. This reaction is a source of energy for metabolism and, ultimately, for all life on earth, since plants are food for all life forms, including humans.

But the plant also breathes, while oxygen is absorbed, which, when combined with a carbohydrate, releases carbon dioxide and energy. The plant breathes day and night, absorbing CO_2 for photosynthesis and releasing it when breathing. As a result, more oxygen is released than carbon dioxide, although oxygen is not released at night.

Gas exchange of the plant is carried out through the pores - stomata, which are located on the underside of the leaves.

In dry, hot weather, stomata close, and the plant slows down metabolism. But even when they are wide open, water vapor vaporized by the plant interferes with the absorption of CO_2. In the hydroponic cultivation method, the root zone has unlimited water supply, the stomata do not close, and a good supply of carbon dioxide supports the plants in continuous growth mode.

When the first plants appeared millions of years ago, the atmosphere was much more saturated with carbon dioxide than now. Perhaps that is why the mechanism of its absorption is imperfect, and additional doses of CO_2 to plants are useful. Increased carbon dioxide helps plants withstand elevated temperatures. Permanent ventilation will ensure the flow of this gas and remove excess moisture.

A piece of rather amusing advice to talk about plants has a practical basis: a person exhales quite a lot of carbon dioxide during a conversation, to which plants respond with active growth. If you want to provide the greenhouse with additional CO_2, you can use sugar with yeast or vinegar with baking soda. You can buy ready-made carbon dioxide in a bottle, although the issue of regulating the amount of gas in the room is not so simple. There are sensors that measure CO_2 and maintain its level automatically.

Frost-sensitive period

Frost can kill a crop or cause serious damage. To some point, severe frosts will even reach the walls of a greenhouse, destroying plants inside. Even plants that are generally frost-tolerant can be severely damaged if the frost occurs at the wrong time of the year: Virtually all fruit or floral buds are susceptible to frosting.

If frost is likely to occur at a time near the opening of flowering buds, fruit development may be stopped even if the rest of the plant is not affected. Frost consumes some young seedlings. Tender, lush young growth is more frost-sensitive. You need to know when frosts are likely to occur at a particular site, and select crops that do not have a high risk of frost damage for that site.

Day length

Day length, along with temperature, is the most important factor for the formation of flower buds and for the development of fruit. For some plants, for you to achieve a good crop, the appropriate sequence of day-length must take place. For other species, there must be a minimum or maximum duration of a day before flower buds develop. For example, of flowering to occur, African violets require at least 16 hours of daylight-or artificial light.

Brightness

The quality of light is just as important for some plants as the duration of the light cycle. Where light intensities are too small, many vegetables and herbs do not achieve the same quality or yield amount. Other plants require lower light intensities and prefer shaded environments.

A hill that receives the midday sun (i.e. north-facing the southern hemisphere) will have higher light intensities than one facing away from the sun in the afternoon. A location obscured by tall trees or surrounding tall buildings will have lower light intensities than one facing off the afternoon sun. A valley site may have lower luminous intensities than one on a hill or flat plain.

Rainfall

There is usually less need to cover hydroponic facilities in low to medium rainfall areas than in heavy rainfall areas, where the runoff will dilute nutrient solutions or leach nutrients out of the system.

The Optimal Temperature in Hydroponics

The temperature of the air is a very important external factor for the hydroponic plant culture site. This factor largely controls the speed of chemical reactions, enzymatic metabolism, and the development of plants (germination, a transformation of vegetative buds into reproductive buds).

The temperature that the farmer must maintain in his space of culture depends above all on the geographical origin of the cultivated plant. Indeed, these have special requirements in terms of temperature throughout their development: for germination, vegetative growth, floral induction.

It should be of note that metabolism is the set of chemical transformations that take place in cells or living organisms. These reactions can be divided into two:

1.) Catabolism - the process of degradation of molecules followed by the release of energy.

2.) Anabolism - brings together the synthesis reactions of macromolecules that demand energy consumption.

How to measure the temperature, what are the biological, chemical, physical processes depending on the temperature and then manage this climatic factor for optimal development of the plants?

To know the temperature in his space of culture, the horticulturist will use a thermometer. Originally, this instrument consists of a glass tube in which expends a quantity of mercury or colored alcohol. These instruments are simple and of sufficient accuracy for horticultural use. However, mercury thermometers can easily break down and spill the toxic metal into the culture space. With high temperatures, mercury vaporizes in the air and can be inhaled by people in the growing space.

Reminder: When an accident occurs with a thermometer, mercury must be collected in a cardboard box, put in an airtight plastic bag and taken to a pharmacist or specialized waste treatment center. Never use a vacuum cleaner to remove mercury from a broken thermometer. (The heat will vaporize the mercury into the atmosphere, it is not eliminated, but it is transferred from the ground to the air...).

The digital thermometers are less harmful to the environment and more convenient for the farmer. The measurement of the temperature is carried out by means of a junction diode in which circulates a constant electric field. The temperature variation of the culture space varies the dynamic resistance of the dipole. The temperature is displayed directly on a screen (LCD) and most of these instruments also indicate the minima and maxima.

Some models have an external temperature sensor (probe) that allows you to know the temperature outside and inside the shelter. This is important for heating management: the greater the difference in temperature with the outside, the more it will be necessary to heat to reach the desired temperature (setpoint temperature).

The best place to place a hydroponic installation is an enclosed space. A basement or a greenhouse is well suited. Also, the hydroponic system can be placed in a small room without windows or in the courtyard of a private house.

The base for the installation of the structure must be strictly even and stable so that the water and the nutrient components present in it are distributed evenly. When installing the structure outdoors, pay attention to the control of liquid evaporation and ensure reliable protection of the hydroponic installation from the wind. Installing the system on the street as a whole is an extremely inconvenient option. In addition, you will have to constantly monitor that the hydroponic installation does not cool down, and bring it into the room even with slight decreases in air temperature. In the case of assembling the system in the house, you will have to make more efforts to organize additional lighting.

Gardening is a field that has developed gradually since the start of time. Since the early days until now, people have tried to develop better techniques to deliver a more effective and easy gardening technique. Different forms and new and better strategies have evolved over the years. Another such method is hydroponics.

Hydroponics helps you to cultivate your plants without any natural hazards throughout the year. Conventional gardening techniques require a number of external factors uncontrollable for plant cultivation.

Incontrollable variables such as different seasons, weather etc. play a key role in yield. Nevertheless, approaches that use water solution instead of soil minimize the risk associated with these variables.

These hydroponic systems can be made in your own home, if you are an experienced plant gardener. You can also go online for the kits made available by the company. Such kits are available in different sizes and can be chosen according to your particular needs.

Such kits include the necessary equipment and elements such as lamps, pumps, containers, nutrient systems, etc. In any case, you will need an in-depth understanding of plants and their different aspects.

There are many different aspects that make the Hydroponics device cycle a success. Lighting is such an important aspect. It is necessary that you give the plants sufficient light to grow.

At least a good eight hours of sunlight should be given to young plants for efficient growth. Remember always that too much is bad. Make sure that light is not too high, especially when using multiple lights.

Other very important factors in hydroponics are humidity and temperature. Each living organism has an ideal level of different environmental conditions, such as humidity, temperature, etc. If plants are grown indoors, it is very important for plants to survive in a good environment.

More carbon dioxide can also be introduced into the plant for better growth. In addition to external conditions, nutrition is equally important. You will be able to better understand their nutritional needs by studying the plants you want to produce.

When you have the necessary nutrient solution in Hydroponics, you must focus on the absorption rate. This ensures that the plant can absorb nutrients without any problems to the best of its ability. The aim of a controlled environment is to be able to change every factor in growing plants to maximize their efficiency.

Air pumps and sleeves can help to improve air circulation throughout the solution. For fact, the water used in the process can also be used over and over again. Whilst it's best to practice gardening before using the hydroponics, beginners can also grow their favorite plants and vegetables in a smaller size.

Hydroponic gardening is nothing other than soil-free planting. It is an economical way to supply plants with food and water. The soil's purpose is to provide plants with nutrients and to protect the roots of plants.

A plant uses food and water in the soil. The plant is supplied with a full nutrient solution and a growing medium in the hydroponic gardening to sustain the root plants.

It allows plants to access water and food more quickly. If you start your first hydroponic garden, a lot of resources and information can be found online. A good way to begin a hydroponic garden is to obey useful factors during gardening.

Some of them are listed below: Grow: you can grow hydroponically vegetables, flowers and medicinal plants. Many of them include tomatoes, peppers, cucumbers, orchids and medicinal plants. You can start a garden by buying seeds online or just buy it from garden centres.

System or method: There are six types of hydroponic systems that you can use for your greenhouse, including Ebb and Flow, Drip, Aeroponic, N.F.T and Wick System. Any device, lighting, and growing medium that suits your plants, garden size and budget can be selected.

Garden area: whether you need a small or large hydroponic garden, you have to decide. The flow of air and the ability to control moisture and temperature in the room depend on your area of cultivation.

Your garden always needs clean water and safe electricity. A continuous water supply with a good pH level is very critical. You need electric power supply for indoor gardening to operate water pumps, grow systems and fans.

Accessories: Depending on the complexity and size of your hydroponic garden, various accessories including light timers, fans, water pumps and meters for temperature and humidity measurement are required. Many hydroponic gardeners will help you to pick different garden needs.

Lighting system: Light is the key component if you plan to start an indoor garden. Understand your growing space and choose the perfect lighting for your garden. You can choose high intensity growing lights that provide sunshine to your indoor garden.

Nutrients: You don't use soil in hydroponic gardening to grow plants. You must therefore provide the plants with full balanced nutrition. Plants require six types of micronutrients, Nitrogen, Phosphorus, Potassium, Calcium, Sulfur, Magnesium, in particular.

A plant needs some small traces of vitamins, iron, boron, zinc, manganese, cobalt and copper. Choose a perfect solution to provide sufficient macro and micro nutrients for your plants.

Growing medium: hydroponic means soilless gardening and therefore soil needs to be replaced by a perfect medium of production. This rising medium provides the plants with nutrients. There are enormous varieties of growing medium that cocoa, organic soil, mats, crushed stones and rock wool can be used.

Hydroponics is not a difficult planting strategy. In this process, the plant nutrients are liquefied during water. A rising medium substitutes the soil for oxygen, water and nutrients to the roots.

The first step in hydroponics is to buy your supplies. The seeds can be put in rock wool starter cubes that fit well into the typical nursery tray. The rock wool should be soaked overnight in a conditioning solution.

Place a seed in each cube.

In each cube. Place the tile under a fluorescent lamp with a semi-circular rim. Wait for the germination of the seeds and for the roots to come out of the cube base. This is the moment when the roots are transplanted into the hydroponic system.

A large yellow pail is required to serve as the external storage that contains the food and water for your plant. The plant actually sits in a small green pail with small pants. More products include fluorescent light bulb, root help marbles and plant food.

Punch small holes in the small holder to prevent too much water from flooding the roots.

Wash the ground from the roots until you see the root system's main part. Handle the roots with great care.

Place some marbles at the bottom of the little bowl. This can be from 1/2 inch to 1 inch to provide enough water and air for proper growth.

Enable the roots to settle at the base to access more water. Fill the bowl with more marbles once this is finished. Inside the larger container, position the small pot until it gets balanced.

You can illuminate the plant to speed up production. Water and feed the plant based on hydroponic gardening standards. Nutrient, salt and water measure. You need one Miracle Grow table spoon, another salt table spoon and one gallon of water.

Combine the solution and pour tenderly on the root until the waterline is almost one inch above the bottom of the small pot in the large container.

Make it a point for your plant to maintain. If the plant leaves turn into another color, a problem can occur. The water should also not be too low or too high. The PH balance is better known. To address this problem, change the water regularly. In any hydroponic supply store, PH level test tools can be purchased.

If you're working to build a sustainable organic garden, try leaving a portion of your garden untouched so that the wildlife will be able to thrive. This is a great natural way to allow the insects and animals found in nature to assist with the growth of your garden.

You must consider how much light is available when starting your plants indoors. The amount of light available can determine which type of organic plants you should grow. For example, if your living area does not provide much natural sunlight, you could grow those plants that only need low to medium amounts of natural light to thrive. If this is not an option, or you have your heart set on a particular type of plant, consider adding additional growing lights instead.

Take your seedlings and saplings to a cooler spot once they are established. To ensure that your plants do not suffer shock, start eliminating the use of a heat source. Remove plastic films on containers to prevent warmth and humidity from penetrating them. Watch your seeds closely to find the right time to do this.

Use about two to three inches of organic material as mulch in all of your flower beds. Mulching is the perfect way to lock in moisture, nourish soil, and to keep away weeds. Also, the flower beds will look beautifully maintained at all times.

Working in the garden doesn't have to be grueling; learn to work more efficiently. Do not waste your time looking for tools. In addition to keeping your gardening tools in one location, you should also clean your tools after each use. You can keep your garden tools in a tool belt, or your pockets. Another good idea is to keep them all in a bucket that you carry around with you.

Make sure you consider adequate spacing when planting your garden so that each plant is given room enough to grow and flourish. Many people underestimate the space needed for plants to grow to their full size. The plants need space due to sheer size and also for air circulation. It is, therefore, important for you to plan accordingly and allow for enough room between your seed rows.

An old laundry basket works great for gathering produce from your garden. You can also use a laundry basket as a strainer. After you have rinsed your produce in the laundry basket, the water will just drain right out the sides.

Your compost pile should contain green plant materials and dry plant materials. Green means plant cuttings including grass, produce and weeds. Dried plant matter, on the other hand, includes shredded paper, used wood chips, and straw. Avoid using animal manure, charcoal or diseased plants in your compost.

Organic gardening may sometimes require more effort than resorting to chemicals, but the payoff, in the end, is well worth the work. While chemicals offer an easy solution to many common gardening problems, the organic method is far healthier for you and everyone you share your food with.

Add mulch to keep your soil healthy. A layer of mulch can protect the soil beneath. It keeps the soil cool on very hot days, thus protecting the roots in the ground. The soil will also stay moist longer because it reduces evaporation. This can also help control any weeds.

It only takes a few simple steps to whip up an amazing garden for all of your perennials. Use a spade to cut and flip over your turf, then cover the new bed with wood chips. Once a couple of weeks have passed, you can then dig into the new garden bed and plant some of your favorite perennials.

Organic material that is a minimum of three inches deep should be used as mulch within your garden. The mulch retains moisture, enriches the soil, and prevents weeds from growing. Mulch also makes your garden appear neat and well cared for.

Create biodiversity in your garden. The more types of plants you have, the more kinds of wildlife you'll have. Plant various plant types to create a natural environment. Different varieties can give you a pleasant garden to relax in while doing good things for the environment.

This tip greatly eases your organic gardening attempts. Bushes, native grasses, and flowers should be the essentials of your landscaping needs. By choosing plants that coexist easily with your soil types, climate, and neighboring plants, you will reduce the need for additional fertilizers and natural pesticides. Native plants will thrive if you encourage growth with organically made compost.

Make Use of a Ph Testing Kit

PH testing kits determine the acidity or alkalinity of the soil which plants grow in the hydroponic system; their use is essential to the nutrient availability of plants. An optimum range for plant soil is 5.5 -6. Which is neither basic nor acidic, but neutral enough for the plant to grow. For plants not to have nutrient deficiencies, the use of a ph system is highly recommended.

Make Use of Water Sprinklers

Ever used a hose to water all the plants in a garden, and you thought that was really tedious? Wait no more for the end to these stressful act, because a tip can literally water your garden without you being there the whole time, and that tip is known as a sprinkler. Sprinklers are an advancement in the hose technology, comprising of a hose that supplies water and a sprinkler common to those found in shower heads used in bathrooms. But here's another tip, these ones rotate, so all you have to do is turn the water supply on and the sprinkler automatically goes 360 degrees watering your plants, while you can do something else.

Apply Compost Annualy to Your Garden

Plants draw nutrients from soil, and this alone reduces the richness of the soil used in cultivating the crops because they deplete with time. One way to ensure that the soil regain these lush nutrients that it once offered your plants, is to allow it either fallow or add compost to it. These ensures the soil is rich enough in nutrients which the plants need.

Think Ahead

Ever heard the quote that says, '' luck is when preparation meets opportunity.'' Then you also should know that a smart gardener thinks ahead. What do you need for your garden to be good? Find out, and get it. What equipment do you need? Also find out and get them. Because the only luck you'll ever experience is when you prepare yourself for the opportunities nature provides you that will make for a successful garden. In essence, think ahead.

Install Garden Netting

Nets are protective covers for young crops from insects, birds and also animals that are more than willing to graze or chew your hard work in their tummies. Animals like cats, sheep and even tiny insects can easily destroy your hard work if you do not prevent them from doing so. And, if you don't want to use a protective net cover. Here's another tip that might prevent any heart breaks should your plants be eaten, don't plant your garden. But, if you intend to, use a protective net cover.

Clean Up Your Garden

Clean your garden, remove any weeds, and leaves that fall on the soil, except you intend using the leaves for compost, but not the weeds.

Prune Your Garden

Ever heard the phrase 'clip your wings'? if you've not, now is the time to know that plants in a hydroponic garden do grow, and can make your garden seem bushy. The best way to cater for this, is to prune your garden. Always use sharp garden tools because they make clean cuts that heal rapidly.

Ensure Your Plants Have Access to Natural Lighting

Plants need natural light to grow because it helps with photosynthesis. If your garden does not have proper access to natural lighting, then they will be deficient, lacking the nutrients photosynthesis offers.

Make Use of Artificial Lighting

Plants need light to grow, so the essentially might not grow as much as they would during the day. The use of artificial light sources such as energy saving bulbs, provide low heat, and a sustainable source that provides the plant some reasonable amount of light which'll enable the plant also grow in the evenings and at night.

Take Extra Classes on Growing a Garden

Take online classes, attend webinars, read books, find out the latest techniques in growing your own hydroponic garden, because this equips you to be at the fore front of planting gardens, and it also equips you with current trends in the business, and also what the future holds. All these forms of information are needed, if your garden will be the talk of the town.

Chapter 9: Mistakes to Avoid

Hard-to-Use Setups

When you are setting up your hydroponic garden, it is important that you consider how hard it will be to use. Are you going to have a difficult time reaching the plants in the back because you put the garden up against a wall? Are you going to bump into the lights every time you try to tend the bed because the space is too small and cramped?

When you are setting up your garden it is important that you consider issues such as the physical space in which it will sit. You want to make sure that you can get to all your plants without a struggle. If you're knocking over lights or throwing your back out to reach plants, then the setup isn't going to be a very good one. Chances are you are going to end up breaking something or neglecting it. Consider the ways in which you move through the garden space; make sure that you are able to reach everything.

You also want to make sure that you are able to get to your reservoir easily. While it may be tempting just to rest the grow tray on top of the reservoir, consider how this might cause issues when it comes time to switch the nutrient solution. Will you have somewhere to place the grow tray while you have to mess around with the reservoir? If not, then how did you plan to do it?

Hydroponic Gardens Are Only for Illegal Substances

It seems that any time hydroponics pop up in the news it is in relation to some illegal grow operation that has been busted by the police. This has led to a stigma around hydroponics, one which it really doesn't deserve. Just

110

because it happens that a lot of illegal growers use hydroponic setups, it doesn't mean that hydroponics is used just for illegal purposes.

As we saw above, we went an entire book looking at hydroponics and never once did we mention any drugs. We looked at how hydroponics will help our herb gardens to produce 30% more aromatic oils. We talked about vegetables and fruits. Never once did we speak about illegal substances.

This is because hydroponics is a system for growing plants. Those plants don't need to be illegal. They can be, yes. But they can also be the garden veggies you serve in a salad. Hydroponics is just a great system for growing plants and it is a system that you can run from inside your house, which means that you can hide your garden easily. But hydroponics itself is not illegal, it does not mean that you are taking part in illegal activities and this particular myth should be put to rest already.

Choosing the Wrong Crops for Your Climate

You hear about a new crop on one of the gardening sites you check online. It sounds like it could be a lot of fun to grow, some kind of berry you never heard of before and people say it does great in a hydroponic setup. You order some seeds, plant it and it grows but it just doesn't give the results you wanted. Looking to see what goes wrong, you do some more Googling on the plant and you realize it needs to be in a super-hot, arid environment. And you're living through the coldest winter of your life.

Different plants want different climates and nothing will be more disappointing than trying to grow a plant that just doesn't like the climate you can offer. We should always do our research on the plants that we want to grow. We can do this easily with Google or by going into our local hydroponic store to speak to the staff.

Myth: Hydroponics Have to be Done Indoors

We've spoken a lot about indoor hydroponics in this book. This was a choice to highlight the fact that we can raise hydroponics indoors. There any many people out there who don't have access to an outside plot in which to start a garden. Most people that live in an apartment building have at best a balcony and many don't even have that much. Being that you can have an indoor garden, hydroponics offers a way for more people to get into gardening.

But this doesn't mean that you can't have an outdoor hydroponic garden. When we raise our gardens indoors, we are able to control the seasons and really take an active role in maintaining the humidity and temperature, how long the grow lights are on and much more. If we grow outdoors, then we can save money on grow lights by using the sun but we also open our garden up to more risk from pests and disease. However, hydroponics can be done anywhere that you want.

Picking the Wrong Plants for Your Setup

This could also be called "Not Doing Your Research." Like picking plants that match your climate, you are also going to want to make sure you pick plants that will work well in your setup. Some plants work better in different systems. Some want less water; some want slower draining and others want more water and others yet want faster draining.

It is important that you research the plants that you want to put in your garden. There are hundreds upon hundreds of websites jam-packed with information about every plant you could consider growing. They will tell you the pH and EC levels for the plant, how hot they like their environment, how much water they want and what type of hydroponic setup is best for them. We looked at a handful throughout this book but there is no way we could have covered all of them. But Google is your friend.

So, make sure you do your research and plan out your garden. Preparing yourself with information will avoid costly mistakes. Not only does it cost to grow but there is also a time cost and you will lose weeks before you realize that growing that one plant is a losing battle.

Myth: Hydroponics is Super Expensive

This myth has good reason to be around. The truth is that hydroponics can be expensive. Can be. But just because it can be doesn't mean that it always is. When you head to the hydroponic store and look at all the prices and get talked into buying more than you really needed, then it is going to be expensive. But like many hobbies, it depends on how serious you want to take it and you can always start slow.

There are a ton of ways to cut down costs when beginning your garden. Searching online you can find hundreds of do-it-yourself guides to starting a hydroponic setup. These offer great ways to try out hydroponic gardening for the new grower. You can get your hands dirty and really see if it is something that you enjoy before you go spending a lot of money. Speaking of spending a lot of money…

Scaling Up the Operation Too Early

Starting off too big can be a terrible mistake. For one, it means sinking a lot of money into growing right out the gate. Before you do this you should at least have some experience with hydroponics. Another big issue is that until you have some experience you don't actually know how to best care for your garden and every step in the operation cycle is going to be a learning experience. This isn't bad when we start small but starting bigger means any mistakes we make along the way are going to cost us that much more.

You should start slow and learn the ropes. As you go along you can buy more expensive equipment as you figure out what equipment you actually need and what equipment works best with your style of growing. As you learn the way your plants take to the system, get a feel for how they grow in your setup, then you can begin to expand. You can start to add in another grow tray, maybe two. But add slowly, take your time and make sure you have a good grasp of how to run a small garden before you jump into a large one. You can always get there but patience will help save you from some truly devastating mistakes along the way. It's one thing to mess up one grow tray, it's another to mess up a dozen.

Myth: Hydroponics is Unnatural

What happened to just stick a plant in the ground and letting it grow? Hydroponics seems like a lot of work to do the same thing. The plants come out bigger, too. Seems like there must be something unnatural going on here. It must be all those chemicals used in the solution.

Of course, this myth is just silly. We are growing plants and using natural mix in our grow trays. We mix together a nutrient solution but all of these are natural nutrients that the plants take from the Earth anyway. Hydroponics is just a system of growing. We grow healthy plants the same as any gardener tries to. There are no gross chemicals being used to give us better growth than soil. All we are doing is using the natural desires of the plant to provide it with the most comfortable growing experience we can.

In a way, hydroponics is almost like owning a pet. There are wild dogs in the world but nobody thinks it is unhealthy to have a pet dog. We are treating our plants the same; we are providing for their needs so that they can focus on living. Just in the case of plants, living means growing into fruit or vegetables that we can enjoy afterward!

Not Maintaining Your Garden

I know, I know. You've heard this one before. But it is the number one mistake that new growers make and so we are going to speak about it one last time. The fact is that maintaining your garden doesn't just mean changing the water. It doesn't just mean we look at the garden when the plants look ill and infected and get to work. Maintaining our gardens is a commitment that any gardener has to honor.

Something spill? Better wipe that up. There's dead plant matter in your grow tray or on the floor around your setup? Best clean that up and get rid of it. Infestations and infections love to grow in these conditions. So, check your plants, test the water, clean up the beds and show them a little love. You wouldn't let your dog sleep in its own waste, so why would you let your plants? Maintaining your garden is the most important thing you can do as a new grower.

Treat your plants right.

Forgetting to Have Fun

If you are growing because you want to sell your crops, that's a fine reason to do it. But try to have fun. For many, this is an enjoyable hobby and brings them a lot of peace. When you start to get money involved, it can be easy to lose track of that. Don't forget to take time to smell the roses. Or the tomatoes, whatever it is you're growing.

Not Doing Any Research

Growing your herbs and vegetables in a hydroponic garden is easy once you get the hang of it. But as a beginner in soil-less gardening, you need to arm yourself with lots of knowledge about the different aspects of a hydroponic garden. Failing to read up on all kinds of information about the different types of hydroponics systems or growing media, for example, can result in your failure to build your dream garden, even if you have all the materials required for the job.

Not Planning for Enough Space

Ensure plenty of space for your herbs and vegetables to grow in. You might try using your backyard's unused shed to serve as a little greenhouse for your hydroponics plants.

Relying on Convenience

Not everything named as a plant food can be used in making your hydroponics herbs and vegetables grow and thrive. You have to realize that nurturing a hydroponics garden is extremely different from tending a traditional soil garden. Aside from taking charge of the proper growing conditions yourself, you also have to take into account the proper ratios involve when mixing your nutrient solution. Always purchase your fertilizer salts and nutrients from reputable gardening centers and other authorized dealers of hydroponics gardening materials.

Depending Too Much on Artificial Lights

Fluorescent lights are not suited for your hydroponics herbs and vegetables at all stages. They are needed most by your seedling plants, which will do extremely well with white light. As your hydroponics plants grow, they would need other light colors (such as blue, red, and orange), all of which natural sunlight can provide.

Neglecting the Plants' Needs for Adequate Air Circulation

In case there is no getting around having to grow your hydroponics herbs and vegetables in a small grow space, consider using a blower or fan to prevent the deterioration of their health due to poor air circulation.

Applying Too Much Fertilizer

Feeding your herbs and vegetables with too much fertilizer only causes salt deposits as well as fungus to build upon your hydroponics system's growing medium. This leads to stunted growth.

Overlooking the Importance of Proper Hygiene

Know that wet floors are a big no in the grow space. The same goes with the accumulation of bacteria in your hydroponic system's reservoir and the presence of any non-sterile equipment or tool.

Harvesting Too Early

While some types of herbs and vegetables can be harvested after only a few weeks from planting, it just might be best for you to allow all your hydroponics plants to reach their maximum growth before you consider harvesting them.

Not Finding the Right Balance

You would not want to neglect your hydroponics herbs and vegetables, either. To achieve the right balance, you might visit your garden and check on its water level, pH level, air circulation, and other hydroponics factors once every two days.

Conclusion

Hydroponics is an economical, environmentally friendly way to grow plants and produce without soil or pesticides. The plants grow faster and produce bigger yields while being completely GMO-free, making them a lot healthier to eat.

Not only does hydroponics allow for fast, efficient, cost effective growing environments, but it is a means to grow produce where it otherwise was not able to grow. Thanks to innovative irrigation systems and the use of various growing media, places that have inadequate soil composition are able to grow fresh produce.

Hydroponics also provides a growing solution for places that have little to no space for commercial growing lands. It has even been successfully tested in space. Hydroponics is not a new concept but has come a long way since ancient times and keeps moving forward in leaps and bounds with new methods being introduced along the way.

It is not a hard concept to grasp and some methods are really easy to learn. There are ready-made kits that one can buy and assemble for each type of system. But they are all capable of being homemade with materials found around the home.

Hydroponics is a great way to teach children the joy of gardening without the mess of dirt and as the plants grow relatively quickly it holds their attention better than normal gardening does.

There are many exciting growing opportunities to be had with hydroponics and if done right, you will be rewarded with bountiful, healthy crops.

Aquaponics adds another dynamic level to the sustainable green farming in that it utilizes natural nutrients generated from a fish tank to organically nourish a media bed. In turn, the media beds offer the fish tank clean water as they filter out all the waste products and return clean water to the fish tank.

written by: © Louis Murphy

A Beginner's Guide to Building a Perfect Greenhouse and Growing

Vegetables, Herbs and Fruit at Home

© Louis Murphy

Introduction

A greenhouse is a structure whose walls and roof are mainly composed of transparent materials, such as glass, in which plants are grown that need climatic conditions. The size of these structures ranges from small hangars to industrial buildings. A miniature greenhouse is known as a cold frame. The inside of a sun-exposed greenhouse becomes much warmer than the outside ambient temperature, thus protecting its contents in cold climates.

Many glasshouses or greenhouses are high-tech structures to produce vegetables or flowers. Glass greenhouses have equipment such as filters, heating, cooling, and lighting, and you can control it by a computer to optimize plant growth conditions. Furthermore, you can use various techniques to evaluate the degree of optimization and comfort ratio of the greenhouse microclimate (air temperature, relative humidity, and vapor pressure deficit) to reduce production risks.

In the seventeenth century, they constructed a greenhouse with ordinary brick or wood, with a normal proportion of windows and some means of heating. When glass became available, and heating forms became more sophisticated, the greenhouse became a glass structure. A considerable increase in the availability of exotic plants in the 19th century led to strong growth of greenhouses in England and elsewhere. Major greenhouses play an important role in agriculture, horticulture, and botany, while amateurs and gardeners often use small structures.

A modern greenhouse is usually a glass or plastic structure to manage vegetables, fruit, flowers, and many plants that require special climate conditions. The basic structural forms are narrow with an A-shaped sloped roof. Sometimes individuals join two or more greenhouses, so there are fewer exterior walls, which reduces heating costs.

Greenhouses have large glass areas on both sides and roof to expose plants to natural light most of the day. Glass is the traditional material, but you can use plastic films, such as polyethylene or polyvinyl, and fiberglass also.

The greenhouse is partly warmed by the sun's rays and partly by artificial means, such as steam, hot water or circulating hot air. As a greenhouse can become too hot and too cold, a type of ventilation system is also needed; they are usually roof openings mechanically or automatically, and the final openings allow electric fans to attract and circulate air throughout the interior.

Each greenhouse model includes some temperature control features and other components to help you utilize the greenhouse's functions. Some of these components or amenities include electricity, heat, water, lighting, shelves, and benches. For example, the heating system enables you to grow your plants at any time of the year, so you don't have to worry about which season is the best for growing each crop. The lighting will enable you to walk into the garden, even in the dark, and work on the crops, including planting new ones, trimming, and cutting.

A greenhouse is a closed space used only for growing crops. Greenhouses allow temperature and humidity to be adjusted in enclosed spaces so that certain crops can grow and thrive regardless of the weather. A greenhouse is an environmental enhancement and strategic planning system that allows the cultivation of plants in climates and seasons that would not otherwise be well suited for their growth

Chapter 1 :Different Types of Greenhouse

It would indeed be a very demanding gardener who would not be able to find a greenhouse entirely like the vast ranges that are now available. There is almost an enormous abundance of choices between the cheapest and the most expensive ones.

Before making this vital decision (even the smallest, most modestly designed greenhouse would mean quite a bit of expense), it is required to discuss the different types of greenhouses in the market and the purposes for which they are most suitable.

Types of Greenhouse

A greenhouse should be placed where it is safe from frost and wind, but away from trees that may provide too much shade and drop leaves and branches on the structure. Find a spot that lets you have full sunshine. The south or southeast part of the building is usually the most desirable location. If this is not feasible, the morning sunlight on the east side may be adequate. Greenhouses with a ridge on top should be built in such a way that the ridge runs from east to west. The site also needs good drainage, even if that means raising the floor so that rainwater and irrigation will drain away. Other considerations include the location of water, heat and electricity. Greenhouses may be purchased in non-assembled kits; prefabricated and ready-to-assembled; custom-designed and constructed by professionals, or constructed by homeowners. Generally, greenhouse forms fall into three groups, with variations.

Span-Roof Greenhouse

The even-sided, free-standing, span-roofed greenhouse is perhaps the most popular type, making it possible to grow as many plants as possible under the best feasible conditions.

There are various variations on the theme, but the span-roofed glass-to-ground-level greenhouses are generally speaking. This type of greenhouse is best suited to average gardeners. These structures are suitable for edible crops, such as lettuce and tomatoes, and for decorative plants, such as chrysanthemums and carnations, which can be grown in beds on the floor of the house. Span-roofed greenhouses of this kind are equally satisfying for growing pot-grown plants on an ash or gravel foundation. The most significant advantage of this type of house is that the plants freeze the full amount of light. It must be said, however, that plants are less quickly taken care of when they are grown on the floor rather than on staging. Furthermore, the heat loss from a full glass greenhouse is greater than when the sides of the house are made of a low brick or wooden wall.

If the aim is to grow plants on staging, then the span-roof house with low walls, as I have just mentioned, is more fitting. This type is a typical span-roof house with a door at one side and staging on each side at the height where the walls end and the windows begin. A useful agreement between the two types already described is the design that allows the glass to be ground on one side, allowing the plants to be grown in beds, and the low wall and the staging on the other side, allowing the plants to be grown in pots.

The Dutch-Light Greenhouse

This type of greenhouse is cheaper to buy than others, as it consists basically of regular Dutch-light panels which are mounted together to make a greenhouse. This type of house is widely used by commercial growers and, in this case, what is good for them is also good for amateur gardeners-but, of course, on a much smaller scale. Today's Dutch-light house was much more draught-proof than its predecessors a few years ago. The lights match tightly together to avoid cold winds, and the roofs are built in such a way as to prevent flooding, which, as any gardener knows, can be as much resented by plants as by draughts.

Another benefit of this type of house is its versatility, as extra lights can be attached to the standard unit to make up a house that is exactly in line with one's requirements (Perhaps 1 can also suggest that some versatility can be built into certain span-roof designs, with extensions available for standard units.) Dutch-lights are made of softwood or Canadian Red Cedar. I would suggest purchasing the latter, although they are slightly more expensive since they last a lot longer and need very little care.

The Lean-To Greenhouse

The lean-to-type greenhouse uses the existing wall, thereby shaping one side of the frame and reducing the cost of materials. Because the wall is usually a house wall, there is likely to be some heat transfer in the winter, which is another benefit. In certain situations, the wall will hold the heat much longer than the windows, and the greenhouse itself will be less open to the elements than a free-standing building.

Like a span-roofed greenhouse, the lean-to-type may have glass to the ground or have a low wall or an embroidered foundation to the height of the staging. This type of greenhouse, a combination of span-roof and lean-to-shaped designs, is not commonly seen today, although it has many advantages. Greenhouses of this sort are designed against a wall like a lean-to-greenhouse, except in this case the house is higher than the building.

The Circular Greenhouse

A beginner in the gardening scene is the circular greenhouse. This offers more space for plants in a given area than other types of greenhouses. In smaller gardens, where space is essential, this could be an especially vital factor. The conservatory or The Sun Lounge, the Modem Sun Lounge (updated conservatory), ideally with access to the living room, has a benefit that is becoming more and more recognized. Many plants which need only protection against frost can be grown in such a structure, and the sun heat will provide appropriate sitting-out conditions for many days in the winter, particularly if there is a steady transfer of heat from the house through an open door or a French window. It is very normal that (the sun lounge remains unsealed except when the weather is coldest, while a small heater can be used to hold the temperature above the freezing mark.

Greenhouse Door Hinged or Sliding?

A lot of the modem greenhouses have sliding doors rather than hinged doors. These may be of great use if space is at a premium. A slight problem with sliding doors, however, is that the base runners can be hampered by grit. Both doors should be wide enough to allow easy access to the wheelbarrow because there are many occasions when this equipment element is required to transport items like manure, plants and flower pots.

There are a lot of considerations to be made before you buy a greenhouse. Obviously, there is budget, but other factors may well influence your budget. If you live in a particularly cold area, then double glazing and heating are important, but in a hotter area, the primary considerations would be air flow and ventilation.

What Size to Buy

Bigger is not always best, but many people aspire to a large greenhouse. What size to buy will depend on the space you have available plus what you are planning to grow. Of course, no matter what size you buy when you start to use it you will run out of space and wish you'd bought a bigger one!

If you are buying a second-hand greenhouse or picking one up for free, then you have less choice in size and will usually make do with whatever comes up.

The most common size is 8' x 6' though you can get slightly smaller ones and very much larger ones. This is a good starter size, but you need to be aware that your space is limited and you will struggle to fit a lot in. However, it is a great size for starting off seeds and growing a few tomatoes or chili plants.

Check any local planning or zoning regulations before you buy a greenhouse. If you are on an allotment, then check their rules too. The last thing you want is to put up your new greenhouse only to find you have breached a rule and then have to take it down. On allotments, you often need written permission for a greenhouse and to position it in a certain way. As to HOA's, their rules are anyone's guess so check and be certain.

I would recommend visiting a shop that sells greenhouses and walking into a few different sizes. This will help you to visualize the space better and work out which one is best for you. Just remember to avoid the sales person's charm, or you may end up with a very expensive greenhouse!

When looking for a greenhouse, you need to consider how easy it is for you to maintain and use the greenhouse. If your greenhouse takes a lot of time to maintain each year, then it means less time doing other jobs.

Positioning Your Greenhouse

Where you will put your greenhouse can influence the size, as well as other factors. Obviously, you need to position it, so it gets good sun throughout the day.

Avoid north facing slopes as the amount of light will not be sufficient. Do not build your greenhouse at the bottom of a slope as it is likely to be the location of a frost pocket, meaning cold air will gather around your greenhouse. This makes your greenhouse colder, requiring more heating and reducing the benefits you get from your greenhouse.

Though if you have no choice but to site your greenhouse facing north that is still better than not having a greenhouse at all!

Depending on your preference you may choose to align your greenhouse in one of two ways.

Firstly, you can align it so the sun tracks down one side of the greenhouse. The advantage of this is that one side gets lots of sun and the other gets less allowing you to grow plants that require less sun or need a bit of shade on the side of the greenhouse furthest from the sun.

Alternatively, you can align your greenhouse, so the sun shines on one of the small ends so the whole greenhouse gets sun throughout the day.

Which you choose is up to you, and it may be that the locations available to you in your vegetable plot influences the alignment.

As an 8' x 6' greenhouse is virtually square, the alignment to the sun is not so important. For larger greenhouses, it does become more important to ensure you maximize the sun for your plants.

Something else to consider is the direction of the prevailing wind in your area. Typically, you will position the door away from the wind. This helps secure your greenhouse and make it a little less susceptible to wind damage. We will talk more about protecting your greenhouse from wind damage later in this book.

You want to position your greenhouse where it is not under trees. Should the trees lose branches, then it will damage or even destroy your greenhouse.

Ideally, you want your greenhouse located in a sheltered spot where it is not going to be subjected to high winds. This may not always be possible, but if you can do this, then it will help prevent damage in the future.

If you are planning on using an irrigation system or installing electricity, then your choice of site needs to take this into consideration. It needs to be somewhere that you can supply these services to without too much work or expense. If not, then you are stuck watering by hand and using paraffin or solar heaters like most gardeners!

All of these decisions need making before you buy your greenhouse and this is probably one of the most controversial!

Which floor you choose will depend a lot on what you are planning on growing in your greenhouse and your environment.

Your choices are:

1. No floor, just use the soil

2. Concrete path down the middle, soil to either side

3. Concrete path down the middle, weed membrane on either side

4. Complete concrete floor

They all have their pros and cons, but it is a personal decision based on your site, budget, and available resources.

Some people do grow direct into the soil using bottomless pots. Just be aware that although this option is cheap, you will be battling weeds inside your greenhouse as well as outside. You also run the risk of introducing soil born pests and diseases if you do not change the top soil in your greenhouse every year or two.

Having a paved path down the middle of your greenhouse is great as it helps with access and isn't too expensive. You can leave the soil bare on either side or cover with a weed membrane.

This method works well, as when you put staging in your greenhouse, it becomes very hard to weed underneath it.

Putting weed membrane down will be effective in keeping the weeds away providing you use a decent quality membrane. Expect to replace it every 2 to 5 years, depending on what you use as it will perish and eventually allow weeds through.

The final option is by far the best but is also the most expensive as you have to buy paving slabs for the whole greenhouse or poured concrete. With a larger greenhouse this can soon become expensive. It is also more work as you have to lay sand and hardcore as well as level the paving.

The advantage of this method is that it is a low maintenance solution. When done properly with weed membrane under the sand, you should get years of a weed free greenhouse.

As everything will be in pots, you can also move your plants around so you can reposition them as necessary to get them more or less sun as required.

Glass vs. Polycarbonate Panes

Again this is a personal preference, and both types of panel have their good and bad points.

Glass is the more expensive solution, and the most fragile, panes can get broken by accident or vandals and need replacing.

However, glass technology is quite advanced, and you can get some great thermally insulated glass which is ideal for colder areas or heated greenhouses.

Most greenhouses use horticultural glass which typically comes in 2' square panes so you can end up with overlapping panes. The disadvantage of this type of glass is that it breaks easily into very jagged and sharp pieces. Because of the size, the panes come in you overlap them, and over time this can become dirty and grow algae, which looks unsightly.

You can buy specially toughened glass for your greenhouse, meaning it isn't going to shatter from a simple touch. It is still breakable, but it will survive an impact from a football though a more solid ball will break it. Just be careful of the edges of toughened glass as that is its weak point. When handling this make sure you never let the edges touch a rough surface.

Plastic or polycarbonate panes are much cheaper to buy and for most applications just as good as glass. The big advantage is that they are a lot harder break which is important if you have kids as accidents do happen.

Because the polycarbonate panes are much lighter than glass, they are also more susceptible to wind damage. In high winds, they can flex and pop out of the frame!

Glass is much heavier and gives your greenhouse a more rigid structure, something that is lacking with the polycarbonate panes.

Many polycarbonate panes are slightly opaque, meaning you cannot see in or out clearly. This may not bother you, but some people don't like it, and it can reduce the amount of sunlight your plants get.

You should also be aware that most polycarbonate panes are twin walled, meaning there are two sheets of plastic with an air gap in the middle. Over time water seeps into this gap and algae forms, which you cannot remove. This has an impact on how much light gets into your greenhouse and also looks untidy. Surprisingly, polycarbonate can cost even more than toughened glass!

Both are easy to get your hands on, being available in many glaziers. My personal preference is the plastic panes purely from the point of view that they are harder to break and less likely to smash if people throw stones at it. However, if I were to heat my greenhouse, then I would look at glass panels for better insulation and heat retention.

Half Brick Greenhouses

This type of greenhouse has several layers of bricks before the greenhouse itself starts. These are not so common these days but are still an option.

Because of the weight, you will need a more significant foundation for your greenhouse. You need to dig down about 18 inches and lay a concrete foundation which will then support the weight of the bricks and the greenhouse itself.

Also known as dwarf wall greenhouses, these harken back to Victorian times when glass was more expensive and brick cheaper. Today, though, brick is more expensive, but the greenhouse does look great and there are some advantages!

The Victorians were masters of engineering and ingenuity, and these dwarf wall greenhouses had a very specific purpose.

The brick heats up slower during the day than the glass which means it helps to keep the greenhouse cool. However, at night the bricks retain the heat and cools more slowly than the glass which keeps the greenhouse warm.

Another advantage is that brick doesn't break. Typically, it will be the lower panes that break as you mow or strim around the greenhouse and kick up stones.

Of course, these half brick greenhouses also look great and are a fine addition to any garden.

Wood vs. Aluminum Frames

Wooden frames look great on a greenhouse, but they are more expensive and will require regular maintenance. You will need to treat the wood every year to prevent it from rotting and keep it looking great. Eventually, though the wood will need replacing and it can be difficult and time-consuming to replace single pieces of wood.

Wooden framed greenhouses look great and when looked after will last for many years. Because of their weight and natural strength, they are less susceptible to wind damage. So if you live in an area with high winds, then it may be worth investing in a wooden frame to prevent damage to your greenhouse.

When you order a wooden frame greenhouse, it will usually come in sections that you put together. For the smaller size greenhouses, it will come as two side panels, two end panels, and two roof panels.

All you need to do is bolt it all together, though you will need help due to the weight of the wood and size of the panels.

Larger greenhouses will come with more panels. You will need to ensure you have suitable access to your greenhouse site so you can get the panels to the right place.

Aluminum frames are much cheaper to buy and will usually come flat packed, so you have to assemble it yourself. They will also usually fit in your car so you can take them home then and there rather than wait for delivery.

This does mean you can do a lot of it by yourself as it is much lighter than wood, but it is also more likely to twist. With an aluminum greenhouse, you need to ensure that the greenhouse is square and level, which can take time.

Although much more affordable than wood, aluminum is a lot lighter. This means you need to take extra care to secure it to the ground to prevent wind damage. High winds will tear an aluminum greenhouse to pieces, twisting the frame and shattering the glass. When properly secured though it can survive all but the most severe storms.

Some greenhouses come with powder coated frames which gives them a nice color. A powder coated frame will last a good ten years without any treatment and can last 15 to 25 years without any need to paint, which surely is good news for us all!

Powder coating is a chemical process which coats the aluminum frame with colored powder. This is baked on. The range of colors available is good though you will need to get your greenhouse from a supplier that offers this service. You can expect to pay a premium price for this coating though.

Which you choose is up to you, but most of us will go for aluminum frames purely from an affordability point of view.

Greenhouses vs. Polytunnels

In many ways, a polytunnel is very similar to a greenhouse in that it insulates your plants from the weather and helps them thrive.

Polytunnels are typically made from plastic or aluminum pipes and covered with a strong plastic sheeting.

These are much cheaper than greenhouses, but they aren't quite the same.

A polytunnel is much weaker than a greenhouse and more likely to be damaged in high winds. It also does not provide the same level of insulation as a greenhouse. It is still excellent for growing plants and keeping them warm, but in the colder months, it will be harder to heat and keep warm.

A lot of serious growers will start their plants off in a greenhouse before moving them into a polytunnel to complete their growing season. Frost tender plants are then often moved back into the greenhouse in winter for that extra protection from the weather.

A polytunnel is a good starter for growing with many similar considerations to a greenhouse. Remember to buy the strongest you can afford and secure it against the wind fully.

Chapter 3 : Health Benefits of Greenhouse Greens

There are a lot of benefits that you get from greenhouse gardening, and not all of them are from the foods you eat. There's a reason I say that it is important to get your family involved in your greenhouse gardening and that is because the act of gardening alone can help improve your overall health — and yes, I am talking about your physical and mental health as well!

You already know — and it goes without saying, but I'll say it anyway — you get a lot of health benefits from growing and eating your own food. Have you ever considered the health benefits you get from simply gardening?

● Your heart health is greatly improved from gardening. Normally an adult should do some moderate exercises at least 3 hours out of every week. You can break this down into 30 minutes of exercise 5-6 days a week. The great thing about gardening is that it gives you that exercise and you didn't even have to lift a single weight to do it. In 2013 a study was released in Sweden that showed results where people who were over the age of 60 but tended to their own gardens had a 27% reduction in risk to damage to their heart. This means they were less likely to suffer a stroke or heart attack (Topping, 2013). No matter your age, gardening is a good way to exercise and it can be done no matter what your mobility is like. When gardening, you also are exposed to the sun more. This increased exposure to vitamin D has been linked to lower risks in bone disease and heart disease.

●Your brain benefits from gardening. A study was conducted that observed and collected data for 3ooo people who were in later stages of life. The results showed that gardening assisted in a reduction of dementia and dementia symptoms by a staggering 35%. Unfortunately, many diseases and afflictions of the brain are ill-understood, so their cures or aids are not well understood either. The current hypothesis on this is that due to the thinking, learning, and problem-solving involved in gardening it keeps cognitive functions alive and working and helps improve brain function. It boosts the quality of life for many patients who suffer from Alzheimer's (Simons, 2006).

●If you suffer from stress in your daily life, then it should please you to know that gardening is considered a huge stress relief. Gardening throughout time has proven to relieve stress that people experience, and this improves overall bodily and mental function. The way that gardening helps you combat stress is through your activity level while gardening and the euphoric feeling of working with your hands and nurturing something to life. As you garden, the cortisol levels drop in your body. Higher cortisol levels are linked to detrimental issues like high blood pressure, joint issues, lower immune system function, heart disease, and a myriad of other health issues. All it takes is a few hours in your garden each week to bring you decreased levels of stress and improve your overall sense of wellbeing.

●Your immune system strengthens as you garden. A lot of this is because you are exposed to more vitamin D and this helps prevent you from catching common colds and the flu. Your immune system is your first line of defense and you need the healthy vitamins that you get from being in the fresh hair and working with the earth. There are bacteria in all dirt, but did you know that Mycobacterium Vaccae is one of the most common strains of bacteria found in your garden dirt? This is a friendly bacterium, so don't panic. It helps reduce your reactions when allergies are introduced. It can also help those who suffer from asthma as well as promote healthier skin.

- Finally, your mental health benefits extremely well from having outside and garden time. In fact, for people who have a history of mental illness, gardening has been used as a positive therapy. It particularly helps people who suffer from anxiety and depression. With gardening, you get to challenge your mind. You also get satisfaction when what you've planned works out well.

Chapter 4: Greenhouse heating, cooling and ventilation process in the details

Heating

In the greenhouse, both heat and light come primarily from the sun. This is particularly true of the hobby greenhouse. A commercial rose grower may have to spend thousands of dollars a week on oil heat in January to get his product ready for the all-important Valentine's Day season, but most of us greenhouses derive 90 percent or more of the light and heat used for growing our plants from the sun.

Solar heat

Your greenhouse should be well designed to maximize the production of solar heat within the building and minimize heat loss at night or on cloudy days. For a discussion of glazing materials, placement of glazed areas, insulation, and caulking, see Greenhouse Basics: Building Your Own Greenhouse.

Preventing Overheating

Heat in a greenhouse is similar to water in this regard: It is more likely that plants will be injured by too much of it than by too little. Any greenhouse, but in particular one that has roof as well as wall glazing, can overheat in the spring and summer months, from April to September. Unless precautions are taken, it is not unusual for temperatures inside such a building to rise to well above 120 degrees, which is hot enough to kill some plants and injure others severely.

There are two ways to prevent overheating. One is to reduce the amount of glazed area; the other, more common, practice is through ventilation. In earlier times, the standard method of reducing the glazed area for a commercial greenhouse, one that is still in use to some extent, was whitewashing. In late spring or early summer, a white compound was sprayed on the exterior of the glass. This material was so designed that a succession of summer rains washed it off; ideally, enough of it was gone by October that it did not need to be removed manually.

Whitewash doesn't work well on glazing materials other than glass, and most hobby greenhouse owners, even those who use glass, don't trouble with it. Instead, they, like the majority of commercial greenhouse owners, cover the top glazed surfaces with shade cloth. This is reasonably inexpensive and lasts several seasons. It is not difficult to apply on freestanding greenhouses, although it may be a pain to work with on attached greenhouses that have a few skylights or an entire glass roof. Some arrangement with inexpensive plastic tarpaulins may have to be worked out for such structures.

Heating in winter

After working all summer to keep the greenhouse cool, the poor greenhouser must work all winter to keep it warm. Rarely will the sun alone suffice. Some artificial heat is necessary, not so much on the coldest days as on the cloudiest ones, and of course at night.

A well-designed attached greenhouse with sufficient insulation and heat-sink material will not need much supplemental heat. If, in addition, there is a system of shutters to cover the glazed area at night, it will need very little. But it will still need some. This supplemental heat can probably be obtained from the house, either through openings or simply by leakage through the wall and glass doors. (It is not only unnecessary but also unwise to insulate the wall between the greenhouse and the house.)

Whether additional heat will be needed depends not only on the construction of the greenhouse, but also on what use you make of it in the coldest, darkest months. If nothing is grown, or if only cold-hardy plants like lettuce and radishes are cultivated, less heat will be needed than if tomatoes or African violets are being grown.

If the plants need more warmth than can be obtained by simply allowing heat from the house to flow into the greenhouse, or if the design makes that impossible, then some nonsolar heat source is necessary. Most artificial heat comes from combustion—that is, from burning fuels like coal, wood, or gas. Combustion gives off gases, many of which are harmful to plants as well as to people.

Electric Heat

The best heating arrangement for a greenhouse involves having the combustion take place elsewhere. Basically, this is what electric heat does, the combustion usually taking place hundreds of miles away or not at all, as when the electricity is generated by water power or nuclear fission. The best heat for a greenhouse or any other building is electric heat, except for one small problem: In most parts of the United States and Canada, it costs much more per unit of heat than burning wood, gas, oil, or coal.

If you need only a small amount of artificial heat for your greenhouse, then it is certainly best to use electricity, in one of three ways. The first, most extensive, and most expensive method is to install one or more electric baseboard heaters. The fact that your greenhouse probably doesn't have baseboards needn't deter you; baseboard heaters don't require baseboards. Such heaters are relatively inexpensive and easy to install. You can do it yourself if you're handy and the local building code permits.

The second method is a small, self-contained radiator. The smallest of these are on wheels so that they may be placed where the need is greatest. They sometimes are filled with water, but more often with oil, which has certain advantages, one being that it won't freeze and burst the radiator as readily as water. They can be plugged into any outlet and include a thermostat, so that they can be set to turn themselves on and off at the greenhouser's discretion. These are extremely popular with small hobby greenhousers.

The third method is the most common and is often used in conjunction with other heat sources. It is a soil or flat heater. In most cases, particularly with sprouting seeds, it is not the air temperature, but the soil temperature, that is crucial. Most garden supply houses stock several kinds of these heaters, and many seed catalogs offer them.

Ventilation

Air circulation is very important in the greenhouse as it ensures that the required temperature is maintained. The amount of air to be supplied per time in the greenhouse depends on the size of the greenhouse, the type of plant cultivated, and also the climatic condition of the area where the greenhouse is set up. The equipment installed for supplying air in the greenhouse should be sufficient for the entire plantation.

The greenhouse environment created for the plants being cultivated is of utmost importance. It is the greenhouse environment that dictates the condition of plant growth. However big or small the greenhouse is, the environmental condition created is what determines the successful cultivation of the plants in the system. This means that you should pay more attention to creating the right greenhouse environment.

Cooling

While ensuring the right growing environment in a greenhouse, the elements can be controlled manually, automatically or through an integrated control system. The integrated control system uses several sensors and computer systems in the greenhouse such that the soil temperature, humidity, air level, and light level are sensed and then controlled as required. In order to maintain the right growing temperature in your greenhouse, the type of temperature control system chosen matters. You should consider the cost of installation and maintenance of the control equipment and ensure that the equipment is able to maintain uniform temperature by regulating extreme temperatures to enhance plant growth. You should also avoid power outages in the greenhouse by putting a backup generator in place in case of power failure at any time. You should also pay attention to the ways through which heat is lost in the greenhouse and replenish them in order to keep the greenhouse warm at the right temperature.

How to maintain the right Temperature in the Greenhouse

Regardless of the size of your greenhouse, the system temperature is one of the important factors that determine successful cultivation. Below are tips on how to maintain the right greenhouse temperature:

1. Install sensors or better yet, monitoring system in your greenhouse. This will help to monitor the change in temperature of your greenhouse. Some sensors will also give feedback on the moisture level of your greenhouse.

2. Ensure sufficient ventilation. The enclosed greenhouse can sometimes create a heated growing environment, sufficient ventilation is then needed to keep the right temperature range. Install cooling systems such as fans or air conditioners depending on your greenhouse size and plant type.

3. Pay attention to your lighting in the system. Depending on the external weather condition, adjust your greenhouse lighting accordingly to maintain the right temperature. Install grow lights if necessary and you may also want to consider installing heaters.

Chapter 5 : Greenhouse Irrigation System

If your greenhouse is in your garden then it is easy enough to pop down and water it, but if it is at an allotment or you are on holiday then watering becomes much trickier, putting your harvest at risk.

In the hottest weather, and more so in hotter climates, you will need to water your plants two or three times a day to keep them healthy no matter how good your cooling system is!

Although you can hand water the plants in your greenhouse, this can soon get boring and difficult to keep up. The best and most efficient way to water your plants is to invest in a greenhouse irrigation system. Which you choose will depend on the size of your greenhouse, what you are growing and whether or not you have electricity and water to hand.

If you are planning to irrigate your greenhouse, then the need to be sited near to water and/or electricity can heavily influence your choice of location.

There are a lot of different irrigation systems on the market with widely varying prices, so you do need to spend some time considering your requirements before rushing out to buy one.

Some plants require more water than others, so depending on what you are growing you may want to get an automatic irrigation system that can deliver differing quantities of water to different plants.

You also want a system that can grow with you as you put more plants in your greenhouse. At certain times within the season you will have more plants in your greenhouse than at others, so your irrigation system needs to be able to support this extra demand.

You do need to be careful because any irrigation system that is introducing too much water to your greenhouse could end up making it too damp, which will encourage the growth of diseases. This is one reason why you need to have your drainage and ventilation right to prevent damage to your greenhouse ecosystem.

You typically have two choices about how to deliver water to your plants, either through spray heads or a drip system. The former will spray water over everything in your greenhouse. The downside of this is that it can encourage powdery mildew on certain plants, but the spray can help damp down your greenhouse. It can also be a bit hit and miss as to how much ends up in the soil of your plants. If you are growing in containers, then a spray system may not deliver water precisely enough.

Drip systems though will deliver water precisely to containers and give each container exactly the right amount of water, so no plant goes thirsty!

The downside of most irrigation systems is that they require electricity, which can be difficult, expensive or even impossible for some greenhouse owners to install. You can purchase solar powered irrigation systems which will do the job, but they can struggle on duller days.

The water will come into the greenhouse with piping and correctly locating this is important. Hanging it from the ceiling and running it along the walls helps keep it out of the way and stops it getting damaged. Running the piping along the floor is a recipe for disaster as you are bound to end up putting a container on it and damaging it!

You will need a water supply and ideally mains water, but you can run some irrigation systems from water butts. You will have to check regularly that the water butt has enough water in it, but it is still much easier than manually watering your plants!

Overhead Misters

If you grow mostly or all one type of plant, then an overhead watering method is a great choice because you can water all your plants evenly and easily. For larger greenhouses, this is a great system because it will water a large area quickly.

The downside of this type of system is that it is quite wasteful of water because the water goes everywhere in the greenhouse, not just into the containers where your plants are.

Your plants end up getting a lot of water on their leaves. If they are over-crowded or ventilation is poor, then this can cause problems such as powdery mildew and make your plants more susceptible to disease.

Mat Irrigation

You can buy capillary matting which works as an irrigation system for your plants. This is a special mat that is designed to draw up water which is then absorbed by your plants through moisture wicks which go into the soil of your containers.

The mat is kept moist by a drip watering system, so you do not have to run water piping throughout your greenhouse. It can just go to strategic points where it feeds the capillary matting.

This is a relatively cheap method of irrigation and is very simple to install. The big advantage is it is very efficient in its use of water, and there is little risk of overwatering your plants!

Drip Tubing

This is special tubing that you run throughout your greenhouse. It has tubes attached to it that run to the roots of each container to supply water directly to the soil. The big advantage of most drip systems is that you can control the amount of water dripped into your plants. This means that plants that need more water can get it and plants that need less don't get over-watered.

This is set to drip at a certain rate or to operate on a timer so it waters at regular intervals. It will depend on the type of system you buy as to whether it is constant or timed. Timed is by far the best as it allows greater control of the delivery of water, reducing the risks of over-watering.

This is a very water efficient method of watering your greenhouse with minimal wastage. It can also be set up to be completely automatic, which reduces the time you spend managing your greenhouse.

With some of the more advanced drip watering systems, you have sensors in the ground that monitor moisture levels and turn on the water when the soil becomes too dry.

If you are growing directly in the soil, then the type of soil will influence your drip rate. A heavy clay soil will take longer to absorb water, so it needs less water than a lighter soil because in clay it will puddle and pool, which you want to avoid.

When you are growing a variety of plants, this is by far the best irrigation method because you can control the amount of water each container receives.

Planning your drip watering system is relatively easy. You need to divide your greenhouse into an equal number of sections, and each area will hold plants with similar water requirements. Depending on the size of your greenhouse you may need multiple irrigation systems, but most are easy to expand with additional piping.

Drip irrigation piping comes in either black polyethylene (PE) or polyvinyl chloride (PVC). These are cheap, easy to handle and bendy when you need it to be.

PVC pipe is often used in supply and header lines as you can solvent bond connections and fittings. Polyethylene connections though need to be clamped. PVC pipe is also more durable, being less sensitive to temperature fluctuations and sunlight but it is more expensive to buy.

Polyethylene pipe is sensitive to high temperatures and will contract and expand. This means it can move out of position unless it is held in place.

Your main feeder piping may be 1" or 2" wide but for lateral, emitter lines ½" piping is sufficient. Each row of plants will have its own ½" line containing emitters. In smaller greenhouses, you can get away with one emitter line for every two rows when plants are spaced less than 18-20" apart.

There are some different types of emitter available. The perforated hose or porous pipe types are very common and are an emitter line with holes in it. The water then seeps out of these holes. Most will deliver water at a rate of anywhere from ½ to 3 gallons an hour. The rate of delivery is changed by adjusting the water pressure.

Alternatively, you can get emitter valves which allows you to control the drip rate for each pot.

Emitters are usually spaced between 24" and 36" along the main lateral lines.

One thing to remember is that you need to filter the water, particularly if it is coming out of a water butt. This will prevent any dirt getting into the system and clogging the emitters. This is vital as it will ensure your irrigation system works without any problems.

Some irrigation systems will allow you to install a fertilizer injector. This is useful as you can get your irrigation system to automatically feed your plants too! Depending on the system this can be set to deliver liquid fertilizer constantly or at specified intervals. This, though, is typically found in more expensive systems, and you need to be very careful in your choice of liquid feed to prevent clogging up the system.

The key with drip irrigation systems is to apply a little water frequently to maintain the soil moisture levels. This is a very water efficient system that is easy to expand and works no matter what size plants you are growing.

Most people who own a greenhouse and install an irrigation system will choose a drip watering system. They are easily available and very affordable though, as with anything, you can spend more money and get more advanced systems.

Chapter 6 : How to clean your greenhouse

Greenhouse cleanliness is absolutely vital. Whether you own a greenhouse, a polytunnel, a cold frame or a portable greenhouse, regular cleaning is vital.

Over time pathogens such as bacteria, pests and fungus will build up in your greenhouse, and these can have a devastating effect on your plants.

When you clean your greenhouse will depend on what you grow in it. If you are only growing plants in the summer months, then you clean your greenhouse in winter, when the crops have all been cleared out.

However, if you grow all year round, then a mild spell in late September or October is the best time to clean. This allows you to put your delicate plants outside while you clean your greenhouse thoroughly. The cleaning also makes sure that your plants get maximum light during the darker winter months.

You will want to put aside a day to clean your greenhouse to ensure you have plenty of time to do the job. Choose a day that is dry and mild, particularly if you are putting tender plants outside.

Firstly, you need to remove your plants from the greenhouse. If you are concerned about them, then cover them with some horticultural fleece to keep them warm.

Then remove any empty pots, the greenhouse staging and as much as you can so the greenhouse is empty.

Your first job is to brush out all the debris from the greenhouse such as soil, fallen leaves and other odds and ends that have been dropped in the growing season. If you have a portable vacuum cleaner, then these are a big timesaver.

Any fallen leaves, particularly from tomatoes and squashes should be destroyed rather than composted.

The internal structure of the greenhouse then needs to be cleaned. Use hot water if you can and try to avoid chemicals which could remain in your greenhouse and harm your plants the following year.

Hydrogen peroxide is a particularly good cleaner that has little impact on the environment. There are specialist greenhouse cleaners on the market and garden disinfectants can be used.

You can use domestic cleaning products, but you need to be careful as these can contain harmful chemicals which can hang around in your greenhouse for months.

Once the structure is clean, then the panes need cleaning. Remove any old shade paint and give them a good scrub both inside and out. Remove any dirt trapped between the panes and, if necessary, remove panes to clean any algae.

Take this time to check the rubber seals and the glass clips on your greenhouse. Any that are perished, broken or missing need to be replaced. Also check all vents, vent controllers, and draught excluders, making good any necessary repairs.

Most Common Vegetables and Fruits to Grow in the Greenhouse

There is a vast difference between the crops grown as starters and the greenhouse vegetables. Masses continue to grow vegetables and fruit in their greenhouses, where they regulate the temperature, provide heat, prolong the growing season and protect them from frosting. However, if you're new to gardening and planting fruit and vegetables, then you need to have good ideas about how to grow in a greenhouse. God has given us countless varieties, so how can you choose the best vegetables to grow in the greenhouse? Just start growing simple vegetables so that you can get your hands on them within a year so that the next season, you can keep growing even the complicated ones.

-

1. Leafy Greens: You have to start with something that belongs to the "salad family" – almost every other leafy vegetable grows in the same way, particularly when looking at bedding green house plants. Other than basic knowledge, some aesthetic knowledge is required when growing leafy vegetables. They have different tastes and colors, making them ideal for starters and sidelines. These can serve as a good source of income, as you can sell them to a variety of grocery stores and even wholesalers.

-

2. Micro Greens: In simpler terms, you will grow up with a lovely look and a mouth-watering taste of Tatsoi, Beet, Peas, Choi and Radish, etc. They are extremely loved as sidelines and as snacks. Once you have good knowledge, you can blend the varieties and make micro-greens of the second generation on your own.

-

3. Spinach: It is one of the best-grown greenhouse plants – if you want to enjoy the freshest and tastiest spinach, take it out of the garden and cook it immediately. It's so safe that you can quickly increase your intake of vitamins and minerals. Most importantly, you're never going to have trouble growing and preserving this greenhouse crop.

-

4. Cucumber: You must have grown up to eat cucumber salads or even raw bits of salt. They taste great – but growing them isn't so simple. You have to shrink wrap them so that they can preserve their freshness after harvesting.

-

5. Tomatoes: Many of the greenhouses have tomatoes in different colors and shapes – especially beefsteak varieties are easy to handle.

Chapter 7 : How to Handle Disease and Pest Control

When setting up your greenhouse and growing your plants, there are some things you have control over and some things you do not have control over. For example, you have control over the watering, and you can even set up an automated system that helps you water the plants at designated times. However, you do not have control over nature; hence, you may have to seek ways to manage it.

Wherever you see plants, you will find pests, but this doesn't mean that you should give up and allow them to ravage your plants. Even if you cannot control the situation 100% in terms of permanently keeping them away, you can manage the situation through effective pest and disease control.

Diseases and pests make your plants vulnerable and will even kill them if they are not kept under control. Pest and disease control is crucial to stay on top of, and there can be cycles that repeat. Even if you fumigate your greenhouse at the start of the planting season it doesn't mean it is safe for the rest of the year.

Pest control is a continuous effort, and it is something you must become intentional about because it determines the success of your plants. You may have some issues keeping the pests away if your greenhouse is located in a pest-infested area. This is why keeping the inside of your greenhouse under control is very important. This is also why you have screens on all windows and vents.

The more you take care of the greenhouse and its surroundings, the easier it becomes to keep the pests away. This chapter provides an overview of greenhouse pests and diseases and how you can manage them. The chapter also provides insight into diseases and covers ways you can keep your greenhouse safe from them.

There are several factors to consider for successful control of pests and diseases in greenhouses, and some of them include:

● Proper cultivation practices that minimize the chance of pests and diseases building up.

● Early detection and diagnosis to enable prompt and effective pest and disease control and eradication.

● The right choice of pesticides and fungicides.

Some greenhouse insects feed directly on plants and some also transmit diseases to plants. Pesticides can be an effective tool for managing greenhouse pests, but most are toxic to humans and can't be used if you are growing organically. As such, if you are going to use pesticides, even organic ones, always follow the appropriate safety guidelines.

Let's highlight some of the common greenhouse pests and diseases, then go over pest and disease control.

-

Some Common Greenhouse Pests

-

Aphids

Aphids are sucking insects that extract the plant's sap, and they are found on the stalks of or under the leaves of plants. They cluster in colonies on the leaves or stems of a plant. Disturbingly, aphids multiply quickly in greenhouses, and can put your entire greenhouse crop at risk if left unchecked.

Aphid infestation often happens when the door of a greenhouse is left open too long. They also get inside through other openings in the greenhouse.

-

Fungus Gnats

Fungus gnats are tiny pests that have long legs and wings that allow them to fly around quickly. The larva of this pest is as destructive as the adult of the species. When fungus gnats infect plants, they start to lose their vigor and begin to wilt.

The fungus gnat feeds on both the plant and the organic matter in the soil. This feeding habit means both your plant and soil are under threat from these pests. The larvae live in soil clusters. Fungus gnats are often a result of overwatering.

-

Cutworms and Caterpillars

Caterpillars are the immature state of moths, and they chew on the leaves, fruits, and stems of numerous plants. A caterpillar infestation starts when moths get into the greenhouse through the ventilators. They also get in though infested plants that are brought into the greenhouse.

Cutworms are a threat to younger plants as they hide in the soil during the day and feed on the plants at night. There are also other forms of caterpillars such as the cabbage looper that feeds on lettuce. You can distinguish it by its pale green color and three looping movements. To monitor your greenhouse for these insects, look for cut plants or leaves that have large sections removed.

-

Mealybugs

These small soft-bodied bugs can ruin an entire plant by sucking the plant's sap. These insects are covered by a waxy secretion that protects them, even from some insecticides. Mealybugs can infest almost any part of any plant. As such, it affects a wide variety of greenhouse plants. Mealybugs also release honeydew secretions on leaves, so if you observe this on your leaves, you can tell when they are in your greenhouse.

-

Slugs and Snails

You will find more slugs and snails in your greenhouse when the humidity is high. They leave holes in the plant, and small seedlings are especially vulnerable to their attacks. If you find silvery, slimy trails in your greenhouse, then that signifies the presence of slugs and snails in your greenhouse.

-

Mites

Mites are very tiny insects that suck out the sap of a plant by piercing the plant's tissue. Despite their tiny size, they are one of the most dangerous and common greenhouse pests. These insects feed mostly on the undersides of leaves, which gives the upper side of the leaves a speckled appearance. When the infestation is severe the plants turn yellow, wilt, lose their vigor, and die. Roses are highly vulnerable to mites, as well as bamboo plants and ivy geraniums. Some bugs may start with one plant and quickly infest the whole greenhouse because the females can lay up to 200 eggs at a time in hot weather.

-

Most Common Greenhouse Diseases

Greenhouses are most commonly impacted by conditions caused by viruses, bacterial diseases or types of fungus.

Viruses

A virus is one of the worst problems because it is incurable. Viruses often present as a mosaic pattern on the leaves. Viruses are often brought into the greenhouse by thrips or aphids, which feed on the plants and infect them with the virus. When you find an infected plant, it should be removed immediately from the greenhouse and destroyed, preferably by burning.

-

Bacterial Diseases

Bacterial diseases include blight and they are also incurable. It is spread from plant to plant on clothing and tools. If you find that plants are getting slimy to the touch, remove them from the greenhouse and destroy them, again, preferably by burning.

-

Fungus

Fungal diseases such as powdery mildew are very common, and can be managed if you can detect them early. Root rot and botrytis are also common and manageable. Sanitation and low humidity are important ways to prevent fungal issues. If you have had an outbreak of powdery

165

mildew, or any plant disease, all pots and tools and the walls of the greenhouse should be sanitized with a mild bleach solution.

Strategies for Pests and Disease Control

Know the Most Vulnerable Plants

Different plants react differently to various pests and diseases and their control measures. This is because plants do not all have the same vulnerabilities and defenses. Of course, all plants are vulnerable to diseases, but some are more vulnerable than others. Get to know the most sensitive plants in your greenhouse and pay closer attention to them, especially in seasons when they are most prone to attack. Additionally, get to know when plants are most vulnerable, for example when they are very young, and right after watering.

Prioritize Sanitation

Your first line of defense against insects and disease in your greenhouse is sanitation. You will have fewer issues with pests and diseases if you can maintain a clean and organized greenhouse. Sanitation isn't an activity to be done only when the greenhouse is messy. You should do it as part of your daily routine. Remember that the cleaner your greenhouse is, the less vulnerable it will be to pests and diseases.

Understand Your Biocontrol Agents

Biological controls help growers a lot, but they are usually only practical at a large scale. These bio-controls help growers by using insect predators to combat the impact of pests in their greenhouses. A good example of this is the use of ladybugs for aphid control.

To understand more about bio-controls, you've got to know the species you are trying to control, including its life cycle and natural predators.

-

Pesticides and Fungicides

There are a wide variety of pesticides and fungicides on the market. You can get chemical blends and there are organic products as well. Some insecticide products are targeted to specific insect pests, and others are just for general use. There are also many useful recipes for homemade pest and disease remedies. As your greenhouse grows and as you add more plants, you will have to increase your knowledge of pesticides and fungicides based on the kinds of plants you grow.

To maximize the effectiveness of insecticides and fungicides in protecting your greenhouse, don't wait until the issue escalates before taking action. Chemicals must be applied carefully and correctly for them to work. Not all of them are to be sprayed all around the greenhouse. Read the instructions and apply accordingly.

The timing for using pesticides and fungicides is also crucial as some pests will only die when you attack them at a particular time during their life cycle. Often, when insects are established in your greenhouse, you can only get rid of them if you attack them from the beginning and repeat treatment over several of their life cycles.

Additionally, do not use only one type of product repeatedly as insects may develop resistance to it, thus making your efforts ineffective. Try out new and useful brands and use pesticides and fungicides that belong to different chemical classes. Group the plant types that are always most infested and monitor them closely while keeping them away from the uninfected plants.

Find out what is available in your area, choose the product carefully and use with caution. You can learn more about pesticides and fungicides by reading about different products online, listening to experts on the subject and interacting with other growers.

-

Learn from Other Growers

Another great way of managing pests and diseases in your greenhouse is to learn from other growers who may have gone through this process and can share their knowledge with you. Always ask them questions about how they handled the challenge and get specific product recommendations from them as well.

Learning from experienced growers, especially those who live in your area, will help you make informed decisions on how to handle pests and diseases. Chances are, what you are going through with your greenhouse may be a challenge they have dealt with. Don't be shy to ask questions.

Have a Consistent Growing Environment

When you have a consistent growing environment, you are more likely to keep the greenhouse free from pests and disease. Consistency avoids fluctuations in water, heating, cooling, air flow and cleanliness. These fluctuations cause stress in the plants, which makes them vulnerable to attack by pests and diseases. Having the same routines will help you quickly detect problems.

You can work with a checklist to help you complete the same greenhouse tasks every day. Even if you get helpers, ensure that they do the same things at the same time every day. When you do this, everything runs smoothly, and the plants have the most stability.

-

Monitoring

One of the best ways of handling pests and disease control is early detection. By persistent monitoring, you will find problems early and be able to make faster decisions about what to do before the problem is out of control. Although you should observe your plants daily, make it a practice to monitor your greenhouse specifically for pests and disease weekly to ensure you spot plants that are compromised.

Pay close attention to plants that are close to ventilators, fans, and doors and inspect the plants in those areas every morning. These are the plants that are likely to be infected first as they are the closest to the points of entry.

You can also use mass trapping tools such as sticky tapes and cards that will trap insects when they get to or near the plants. If you monitor consistently, you will prevent a lot of pest infestations and diseases.

-

Essential Cultural Controls

Pests can get into your greenhouse on new plants, but some others may get in through open ventilators. You can protect your greenhouse from these pests through cultural controls such as:

169

- Find and remove infested plants from the greenhouse.

- Maintaining a weed-free greenhouse.

- Avoiding overwatering and high humidity.

- After every production cycle, clean the greenhouse thoroughly.

- Always scrutinize new plants before taking them into the greenhouse.

  -

When you deal with pests and handle disease control effectively, your greenhouse will become an ideal environment for your plants to thrive. You will find that you have healthier plants, and this will directly result in bigger yields.

Consistency and diligence are the key to preventing and eradicating greenhouse pests and diseases. If you are not consistent, you may have great results for a little while and then struggle with ongoing problems. However, consistency makes it easier for you to establish a healthy routine and set yourself up for success.

-

Chapter 8: How to Grow Great Yields All Year Round

-

With a greenhouse, you have a unique opportunity to plant and get exceptional yields throughout the year. However, the fact that it is possible doesn't mean everyone experiences the same success. Some growers try so hard and still struggle to effectively grow crops because they haven't learned everything they need to know.

With every general topic you have learned thus far, there have been steps offered to guide you and to help you get it right. In this chapter, you will also learn the key steps to follow to maximize your experience and success in the greenhouse. You will gain insight into how best to achieve the highest yields in your greenhouse all year round.

Some growers complain about the inconsistencies they experience with the planting process. They have excellent yields one season and bad crops the next season. Such a variation in success can be very discouraging, and it can make the grower give up entirely.

However, this is not to say that there is a fool-proof way to have a challenge-free planting experience. Challenges are a reality of greenhouse gardening. Despite those challenges, there are ways to improve your chances of success. You have already learned a lot of them. This chapter offers even more insight into the steps that successful gardeners rely on to improve their yields and overall growing experience.

-

How to Achieve High Yields from Your Greenhouse

-

Start by Growing What You Love

When you are ready to plant your seeds, you will have a myriad of options to choose from. This can be overwhelming at first, so the natural way to focus your energy is to start growing what you love first. Of course, you can always broaden your scope to include other plants as time goes on.

Starting with what you love or enjoy most will help you get used to the process faster than anticipated. After perfecting the process with the crops that you like, you can take on more challenging plants and excel with them too. You can also start with vegetables you may have enjoyed in the past, or that are more expensive to buy than other vegetables. The whole idea as a beginner is to start with easier plants and gradually expand the varieties you grow when you have some experience.

For example, if you really like broccoli, you may have been reading a lot about broccoli, and you may now know a lot about it and want to try to grow it. Since you know how to grow it, its ideal temperature, soil type, nutrition, watering, pest control, etc. this means that planting broccoli will be easier for you. Research always helps, and it is always more interesting to learn about things you like! Once you've done a bit of research, get some hands-on experience by growing that item.

Make a Plan

Next, you have to have a plan for what you want to plant. By now you have likely decided if you will buy starter plants or plant seeds. This may be influenced by budget or availability. Knowing what you want to plant and how much room you have is your starting point. Learn about the plant's growing habit, especially if you are starting from seed. If you have starter plants, you will not need this information about seeds right now, but you may need it later.

All seeds are NOT the same. If you are going to plant several types of seeds, make sure you know the specific requirements for each of them and work towards using those specifications.

Then create a planting plan that details when you will plant the seeds, when their different growing milestones should be anticipated, how you will monitor and groom them, and any special needs they may have between planting and harvest time.

Planning helps you identify what you must do to get exceptional yields and keeps you focused on it. When you don't plan, it becomes easy for you to assume that everything will get done, but the truth is, you are likely to forget some things, or put them off. You need to work diligently and according to a plan to ensure that all aspects of the planting process are productive.

-

Create the Perfect Growing Home

Ensure that your seeds are planted in healthy and fertile soil, since it will be home for them until they grow to full size and get harvested. Once again, check the soil viability by checking temperature, getting rid of pests around the soil area, and ensuring the soil has been properly prepared.

This means that before the seeds get put into the soil, you may have to make some changes to the temperature and humidity inside the greenhouse, and you should water the soil thoroughly. Just like you make your new house comfortable and safe for yourself, you need to ensure your greenhouse is comfortable and safe for your plants. This is the new home for them, and ensuring it is as perfect as possible will ensure the best yields.

-

Test Your Seeds

Before planting your seeds, you might want to test them to be sure that they will germinate when they get into the soil. This testing process is crucial especially if you are using old seeds. If you buy the seeds from a store, check the date on the package to see how fresh they are. Fresh seeds have a very high germination rate, and the germination rate decreases as the seeds get older. Use the best quality seeds you can. The seed germination test is straightforward and has only six steps.

-

Step One: Get All Materials

You will need:

- Ten seeds of all the types you are testing

- One or more Ziploc bags

- A few paper towels

- Permanent marker to label the Ziploc bags

-

Step Two: Wet the Paper Towels

Now dampen the paper towels and spread them on the counter.

-

Step Three: Place the Seeds

Put the seeds on the paper towel and space them out so they don't touch. Do not mix seeds. For example, put all tomato seeds on one paper towel, and put another kind of seed on another paper towel.

Step Four: Seal Seeds in Plastic Bags

Roll the seeds inside the paper towel and press it gently to make sure the seeds firmly touch the paper towel. Place the paper towel wrapped seeds inside the Ziploc bag and seal it. If you are going to test multiple types of seeds, repeat the process and write the plant type on the bag with the permanent marker.

-

Step Five: Wait for Germination

Put the sealed bags in a warm spot in your house and wait to see if they sprout. Be patient. Some seeds take only a few days to sprout, but some take up to 10 days or more.

-

Step Six: Check the Seeds for Germination

Every few days check the seeds for germination by carefully unrolling the paper towel. If they haven't sprouted, roll them back up, put them back in the bag and tuck them back into their warm spot. When you open the towels and you see the seeds have germinated, count the number that have sprouted and multiply that number by ten; this will give you the percentage of germination.

For example, if 6 of the ten tomato seeds sprout, then it means you have a 60% chance of germination when you plant those seeds. The testing process is crucial because it prepares you for what to expect from the seeds and lets you know how much space to allocate to that group of seeds.

Planting

After testing the seeds or acquiring your starter plants, you can then plant them, and this is an easy task to complete. Simply place the seeds or plants into little holes in the ground, in the pots, grow bags or raised beds. After putting them in the holes, cover them with more soil. If you are planting seeds, check the packet for additional instructions.

Then place your water dripper by the plants so the plant can get its first taste of water. You don't want to flood the seeds, so don't overwater at this stage. Now you can put into practice all you've learned about watering, temperature, etc. This is the time to put all those lessons to work by ensuring that the plant has the best chance of success. Remember that if you are using a pot, then it will need more water than if you are planting directly into the soil.

-

Stringing or Supports

If the crops you plant will grow taller as time goes on, then you have to string them up or provide other supports. Stringing or stakes support the plants as they grow. Every plant should have its own string or stake, which guards it against growing into nearby plants or falling over.

In some greenhouses, the growers may not use strings or stakes; they may use some other creative tools to separate the plants and support them as they grow. You have to keep taller plants apart so they can have enough air flow between them. When taller plants have no boundaries, they become too difficult to manage, and their ability to grow well is affected.

Plants like peppers, tomatoes, and beans all grow tall, and they need supports. Ensure that they don't fall over or are not pressed against other plants.

Check Your Plants Until Harvest

Keep an eye on your plants as they grow, and watch out for changes, growth, and signs of any problems. The fact that you got the initial planting process right doesn't mean you should leave the plants and just hope that they grow. Remember all you have learned about pests and disease control. Monitor your plants every morning when you water. Soon you will see them sprout and open up into leaves, stems, roots, fruits, and flowers.

Watching plants grow in a greenhouse is such a fulfilling experience. At this point, you should know that all the plants you planted may grow and yield at different times even though you planted them at the same time.

Monitoring is also crucial for exceptional yields because it helps eliminate threats that may try to kill the plants. If you can catch a bug or mildew problem early, you will have a better chance of your plants making it to harvest.

Every plant has its growth duration and estimated harvest time, and you should know this information for every plant in your greenhouse. As the plant gets closer to harvest time, you should see all the signs of maturity and know that it will soon be time to harvest the fruits of your labor.

When the fruits and vegetables are ripe and ready, hand-pick them immediately. If some fruits are not yet mature, leave them for a while and come back later to pick them. Wash your harvested food with water and enjoy your yields!

Organic Fertilization

Just like plants need water, they also need food. A good quality soil will have lots of nutrients in it, but as the plants grow, they will use up the nutrients that are available. For this reason, you may need to enhance the soil with fertilizer. Fertilizers can be essential to success. The focus here is not on chemical fertilizers, but on the viability of organic fertilizers. Chemical fertilizers can cause harm to your greenhouse plants and to you if they are incorrectly used.

This is why you are advised to focus more on organic fertilizers that are natural and harmless to your soil and the plants. The organic fertilization process will help you plant and grow crops safely while giving them the boost they need to thrive in your greenhouse. When you go fertilizer shopping, insist on organic brands. If you don't trust the products available at the store, you can create your own organic fertilizer if you have the supplies available.

There are tons of resources online that you can use to learn about creating organic fertilizers suitable for all soil and crop types. The natural process may be a lot of work, but it is worth it as it will help your plants grow healthy and have the best yields.

-

Consistency Counts

As you have already learned, when it comes to planting and growing impressive crops, consistency matters. Always strive to provide a consistent growing environment for your plants. If you try a particular planting style and it worked for you, why don't you use it again with the same plants? By repeating a successful planting trick, you will likely achieve the same results consistently without fail. Of course, all the conditions have to be the same, including the same type of soil, temperature, timing, etc.

To use this rule of consistency, you have to be very observant when planting, as this will help you know what you did so that you can achieve the same results. Consistency works when you plant the same crops over and over again.

For example, if you always plant tomatoes, after your first few tries at planting and getting good vegetables during harvest, you will know what to do the next time you plant. But if you have never planted cucumber before, you may have to take time to learn how it works before you can achieve a good harvest. Similarly, if you have a crop failure, try to understand why it failed and avoid doing the same things next time. Keep working at it and be consistent. This is the surest way of getting exceptional yields.

-

The planting process itself is never the same for all plants in your greenhouse. Sometimes, you will have it easy, and other times you will be required to work extra hard, especially when the weather becomes a challenge. The best way to consistently enjoy yields is to keep on trying because the more you try, the easier it becomes for you.

Most of the experienced and talented growers gained most of their knowledge by making mistakes and trying again and remaining consistent in their efforts even in very challenging times. Don't give up!

Chapter 9 : Common Greenhouse Gardening Mistakes and How to Avoid Them

We have had a lot of time to perfect and work on our greenhouses. The first real greenhouses were seen roughly 700 years ago. The Vatican built the initial structures so that rare and exotic plants could be preserved and studied as explorers came back home from their travels. Today, the greenhouse has expanded to be a need for most gardeners rather than a luxurious want.

The greenhouse works because it holds in the sun's heat and creates an atmosphere that is ideal for plants that require warmer temperatures and climates to flourish. It will take you some time and a lot of patience when you first take up greenhouse gardening. As a novice, there are countless mistakes that can be made.

1. The temperature isn't controlled. Often, you can get so used to the idea that your greenhouse is regulating its own temperature because of your controls and systems that you forget to check-in and make sure it is functioning correctly. You should still check in on your temperature every day. Summer temperatures for a greenhouse lie between 70°F to 85°F during the daytime. Your evening and nighttime temperatures will generally fall to between 60°F or 75°F. These temperatures will lower in the wintertime. Your day temperature in the winter should be between 65°F to 75°F and your evening temperatures should be around 45°F to 50°F. Make sure that you are using your ventilation systems, shade cloths, and heating systems to accurately control your temperature in your greenhouse. It's easy to avoid this mistake if you are diligent. Keeping an eye on the temperature is as simple as hanging up a thermometer in your greenhouse. If you have the spare cash, you could even buy a digital thermometer that includes your humidity levels.

2.   Humidity goes uncontrolled. It goes without saying that humidity is a simple part of your greenhouse water cycle. Your plants will bring water to their vital functions through their roots and then this water gets transpired into the air. Air has its limits and capacity, so the air can only retain so much water. If the temperatures in your greenhouse are constantly fluctuating, then it can cause serious diseases and even damage your plants. Your humidity levels fluctuate a lot if your temperature is fluctuating a lot and you don't want that to happen. There are expensive systems you can buy to monitor your humidity, but if you keep a vigilant eye on your temperature you can avoid that extra expense. As the day gets hotter in the summers, make sure that you ventilate your greenhouse so that it doesn't receive a sudden spike in temperature. If you know it is going to be a cloudy day or before the end of the day make sure you have your ventilation system closed off so that your greenhouse temperatures don't drop drastically. You want to avoid dew droplets from appearing on your plant's leaves. So, investing in that digital thermometer can help you keep a good eye on your greenhouse temperature and humidity.

3.   Another common mistake that greenhouse gardeners make is to forget about the trees growing close to their greenhouse. Often a greenhouse is built in the wrong area of a yard because the trees were not taken into consideration. There are two faults with placing your greenhouse close to a large tree. Trees bring shade to your greenhouse and this can negatively affect your plants and the temperatures in your greenhouse. They also have a lot of falling debris — leaves, and if you're particularly unlucky fruit and sticks — which can hinder the sun from getting into your greenhouse. This means that you will have to put a lot of extra legwork into removing the fallen debris so that your plants can get light. If a branch falls onto your greenhouse then there is a chance it can damage

it and you don't want that either. The third issue with having a tree close to your greenhouse is that the roots can become invasive and creep into your greenhouse from below. This can take away precious nutrients and minerals that your plants need to survive. As you are getting ready to build, keep the surrounding trees in mind and make sure that you either remove problem trees or place your greenhouse in a different area. Pruning back problem trees can also help with shade problems.

4.   One of the more common mistakes that can be made no matter your experience in gardening is to over or under water your plants. Your greenhouse will preferably be set up with a drip irrigation system to ensure that all of your plants get the water that they need, however, this doesn't mean you shouldn't monitor your plants. If you don't use drip irrigation, I suggest you keep a closer eye on the plants to ensure they are well watered. Humidity can affect how much water your plants need so it is important to remember that watering your plants involves more than simply watering them with the amount of water that the instructions give you. I suggest watering in the morning to avoid this issue and gauging your plants closer to the end of the day. Is the soil dry or is it still moist? Young plants that haven't matured yet will require more watering throughout the day — especially in the hotter months. A good sign to see if you're under-watering is that your leaves will wilt and turn yellow at the bottom of your plants. Give your plants an extra drink. Luckily you can often correct watering issues fairly quickly if you watch for what your plants are trying to tell you.

5.   While too much shade can be a problem for your plants, forgetting to provide shade to the plants that need it can be an issue as well. This is where getting to know your plants well comes in handy. You can control shading through the use of a shade cloth in your greenhouse garden.

During the summer months, it can be difficult to regulate your greenhouse temperatures, especially if you're new to greenhouse gardening. You can use shade to your advantage to cool down your plants before the heat has a chance to destroy them. If you make sure that your ventilation system works well and you make proper use of your shade cloth (for example, tomatoes are often a vegetable/fruit that require some shade) then you can save water and save your plants. You save water because if your plants are not heat stressed then they won't require as much water to survive. You can get a shade cloth at most garden centers and nurseries. They work by blocking the solar radiation that comes in from the sun.

6.   Limiting the light that your plants receive is another common error you want to avoid. Obviously, there are instances when you have to limit light and you employ your shade cloth in those circumstances. However, sometimes there are key things we are missing in our greenhouse that make us blind to the ways we are detrimentally limiting light for our plants. When you start deciding on which greenhouse material to use for the covering you will notice they all have a rating for the transmission of light. normally your plastic sheeting will be between 4-6mm. The 6mm sheetings are normally your most durable for plastic sheeting and they are typically followed with a rating of 9% for light transmission per layer of sheeting. Obviously as time goes on, your sheeting will age and it will degrade a little bit. This means that your light transmission will go down. There are ways to keep track of the light in your greenhouse by buying a solar power meter, however, that is not necessary. Keep a close eye on your plants and make sure that they receive all of the light they need by keeping an eye on your greenhouse covering. If you use a covering like a polycarbonate plastic or glass covering, then you also have a chance of limiting light exposure. You want to make sure to keep dirt and

grime off your greenhouse coverings so cleaning your glass windows or polycarbonate covering every now and then will be a prevention against limiting light exposure. This situation can get pretty dire and, in some cases, you could be preventing over 10% of light rays from reaching your plant.

7.   Ventilation is very important however, it can also be a finicky aspect of greenhouses to learn how to control. Relax if you're struggling with this — all gardeners do at some point. You learn more when you're relaxed than if you let common mistakes plague your mind. You want to be able to balance the temperatures in your greenhouse by using ventilation. More often than not you will find your ventilation system is inadequate if you're having ventilation issues. A good way to decide how much ventilation you need is to count up your total floor space in the greenhouse and then divide the space by 5. Your ventilation should be roughly 20% of your floor space. This means that 20% you calculated is the lowest area percentage that you should dedicate to windows that open, roof vents, floor vents, or even walls that roll up (this depends on your covering). Airflow is an important aspect that is often forgotten when it comes to ventilation. Opening a window is great, but what happens if there is no breeze that day? Your plants need fresh air to flow throughout the greenhouse. Airflow issues can easily be solved by placing a fan in your greenhouse which will keep your air flowing and moving.

8.   Sometimes we can forget to check on how we manage our soil in our greenhouse gardens however, it is important to remember that soil issues work similarly inside a greenhouse as they do outside. Here's the thing, you're normally going to use the same area to continue to grow similar plants in your greenhouse again and again. When you continue to use the same plot of soil for

replanting it does three things to your soil: it loses fertility, ends up being compact, and becomes a haven for the pests you want to keep out of your greenhouse. If you're preparing your plant beds, a good idea is to use a blend of soil mix which you can easily purchase from a nursery. Also, make sure that you add both fertilizer and compost routinely to your soil beds so that they maintain their fertility. Avoid using old potting soil that you have lying around because you heighten your chances of getting pests and infections in your greenhouse. Make sure you're using a good quality compost in your soil because this can help you achieve the right levels of moisture and nutrients in your soil. Your plants will thank you in the long run.

9.   Inadvertently, gardeners can sometimes encourage fungus to grow in and around their plants. The reality is that your greenhouse is a warm place with a lot of moisture in the air. If you don't control this then your greenhouse climate can become the perfect place for both fungus and mold to set up their homes. For example, with a humidity percentage over 85% and no airflow in your greenhouse, any water droplets that accumulate on your plants will turn into mildew. The best thing to do to avoid making this mistake is to encourage airflow throughout your greenhouse and keep enough space between your plants so that air can flow through them all. The other thing to do is to thin out some of your plants and bushes so that moisture doesn't get trapped inside the plant's leaves and stems. Avoid watering on top or over leaves and buds of a plant, try your best to only water the soil by the roots. Drip irrigation can help ensure the right area of the plant is always getting watered. The most common fungi that you will be trying to prevent are mildew, black mold, and grey mold. These show up in the form of root rot, spots on leaves, and decay in the plant. Bear in mind that it is up to you to watch and know your plants to prevent fungus from spreading. Make sure that you regularly clean your

greenhouse and the tools that you garden with. This way you don't inadvertently spread fungus around. You can use a simple vinegar solution to clean your tools.

10.   Your greenhouse is a warm environment and not every plant loves to thrive in such warm environments. Sometimes you can end up planting the wrong plants inside your greenhouse or starting your plants too early in the season which leaves your greenhouse too hot for them to grow properly. This is where you need to keep in mind the needs of your plant and what you can provide for it and when you can provide it. Your goal is to ultimately extend the seasons for most plants in your greenhouse and possibly have some things grow year-round. A good practice is to start your vegetables during winter and start your seedlings as the temperature gets warmer for your other plants.

Avoiding mistakes is what we all seek to do, however, the reality is that mistakes are a part of human nature. You can't run from them, nor should you want to. If you make a mistake, then take a deep breath and problem solve instead of panicking. You'll learn a lot this way and you will be grateful for it. Besides, sometimes the best things are born from mistakes.

Chapter 10: Useful Tips for Better Production

Some quick tips that will help beginners to grow and get better profit from the crops are as following

Find your market

- Secure labor

- Develop a pollination plan

- Pest Control

- Access your irrigation plan

- Check your progress

- Analyze your product

- Take notes for future projects

Vegetables That Require Wet Soil:

- Leafy Vegetables: Green vegetables that are high in nutrients will grow exceptionally well in wet soil. Such as spinach, butterbur or kang kong.

- Sweet Roots: Vegetable more along the lines of a carrot, try skirret also do good in wet soil.

- Peas

- Lentils

- Fava beans

- Beets

- Cucumbers

- Peppers

- Squash

Vegetables That Require Less Wet Soil:

- Zucchini

- Lima beans.

- Pole beans.

- Corn.

- Cowpeas, black-eyed peas and field peas.

- Edible amaranth.

- Quinoa.

- Mustard greens.

- Okra.

Conclusion

The greenhouse is a system of change and management of the environment that allows plants to grow in climates and seasons that otherwise do not fit well with their growth. It is an environment in which you can control the factors that promote the growth of plants. Factors such as heat, humidity, ventilation, sun, etc. These factors and many others determine the quality and quantity of their performance.

The construction and design of a greenhouse should be made based on these factors because they can determine the optimal greenhouse performance.

Make sure the site has easy access to the water, electricity and other necessary public services. High, stable soil is needed to avoid unnecessary water accumulation. Find a place where there is decent ground for growing plants or the potential to grow. Expandability must also be considered.

Greenhouse plants are exposed to many pests and diseases. In addition to the particular problems of plants, some many pests and diseases attack plants in greenhouses. Therefore, health and control of pests must be carried out. Insects such as aphids, whiteflies, leaf miners, etc. affect performance in a greenhouse.

The list of pests above may seem painful or even frightening, but remember that this is an exhaustive list of major pests. It's unlikely you'll get them all. You can go years without it. It is better to be prepared. If you know how to recognize parasites and fight them, you've won the battle.

Many problems with pests and diseases caused by the greenhouse effect can be greatly reduced by only observing a good cleaning practice. Always remove all old plant materials and greenhouse composts, and whenever you use a knife to cut or remove damaged plants, always clean these tools with a good garden disinfectant. Also, always keep very strong chisels and pruners, as this will reduce damage to plants, which can cause infection or pest attack.

The area around a greenhouse should be kept relatively free of weeds and plant material that can carry pests. This can be done with winter fabric or a plant covered in a barrier at least 10 feet wide around the structure. Preferably, an area with grass should be maintained beyond this area.

Pests often enter the main entrance of a greenhouse because it is the path of least resistance. A lock entry is essential in greenhouses equipped with fan and pad ventilation systems. An airlock can only be obtained by installing a room that locks the door of the greenhouse.

Greenhouse gardening offers many benefits that go beyond the benefits of conventional gardening. One of the main benefits of growing greenhouses is that they offer a longer growing season. Temperatures do not vary so much in a greenhouse because solar radiation is trapped within the enclosure, which retains heat in the structure. The growing seasons can be extended even in cold climates.

With a greenhouse, you don't have to worry about the weather because everything is covered. Even if it is raining outside, you can garden and stay dry. You have the opportunity to grow a variety of plants when using a greenhouse. It allows people to experience exotic plants that are not found in the area.

© **Louis Murphy**

CPSIA information can be obtained
at www.ICGtesting.com
Printed in the USA
LVHW021322091120
671125LV00003B/381